For Neil, and for all the wild campers –
past, present and still to come – this one's for you.

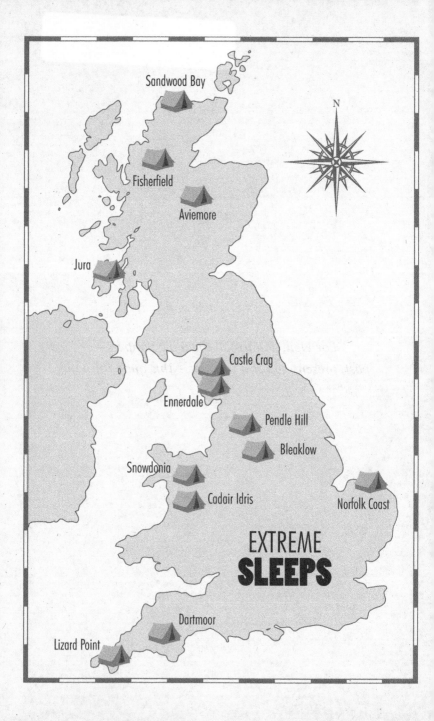

EXTREME SLEEPS

ADVENTURES OF A WILD CAMPER

PHOEBE SMITH

summersdale

EXTREME SLEEPS

Summersdale Publishers Ltd
46 West Street
Chichester
West Sussex
PO19 1RP
UK

www.summersdale.com

Printed and bound by CPI Group (UK) Ltd, Croydon, CR0 4YY

ISBN: 978-1-84953-393-5

Substantial discounts on bulk quantities of Summersdale books are available to corporations, professional associations and other organisations. For details contact general enquiries: telephone: +44 (0) 1243 771107 or email: enquiries@summersdale.com.

CONTENTS

ABOUT THE AUTHOR

Phoebe Smith's love of dramatic landscapes has taken her on backpacking adventures all around the world – from wild camping on the Scottish islands, sleeping under swag in the Australian outback and watching the Northern Lights from a heated wigwam above the Arctic Circle. As a Travel, Adventure and Outdoor Journalist she has regularly written for a number of newspapers and magazines in the UK and overseas and is the author of *The Camper's Friend* and *The Peddars Way and Norfolk Coast Path* guidebook, published by Cicerone. She is currently editor of adventure travel magazine *Wanderlust*.

'*Whatever special nests we make – leaves and moss like the marmots and birds, or tents or piled stones – we all dwell in a house of one room – the world and the firmament for its roof.*'

John Muir

INTRODUCTION

It all started in Woolloomooloo during an argument with an Australian. With the World Cup in full swing, blaring out from the one tiny, flat-screen TV nestled behind the bar, the place was rammed full of Aussies hopeful that tonight was their night. During the half-time reprieve I had unwittingly struck up a conversation with one of them who, after establishing me as a Brit aka 'the enemy' (for that night at least), proceeded in typical pom-bashing fashion to list all the reasons why Oz was better than the UK. And I was countering every one of them – or trying to, at least. When he mentioned the Sydney Opera House, I knocked it back with Big Ben. When he cited the Harbour Bridge, I could easily hit back with the Tower of London. But when he brought up Ayers Rock, I found myself at something of an impasse. Sensing a weakness, he hit back again with the Blue Mountains of New South Wales. When I had still failed to come up with a counter argument, he finished me off with the Great Barrier Reef.

I felt like a failure – as a Brit and also a traveller. Here I was, hundreds of thousands of miles away from my home country and unable to think of a single natural landscape that draws tourists to its shores. I knew they were there, of course I did, I had grown up in North Wales with the giant Snowdonia National Park at my door. But other than going there as a child, forced by my parents while staging a melodramatic protest at having to leave the car and actually walk, I had never been as an adult and consequently couldn't name any particular highlight with any authority.

Up until that point I was as guilty as so many of us Brits are – I had taken our home country for granted. 'Why go to Scotland when I can go to Saigon?' was the mantra of us backpackers, when really it should have featured the additional line (as completely unglamorous as it may sound for a wide-eyed twenty-one-year-old): 'Or I could go to both.'

Over the following months after my bar-room argument, I made my way in almost meticulous fashion all over the land Down Under, taking part in activities alien to me back home. Eventually I made it to the aforementioned Ayers Rock (or Uluru), where I walked for hours around the mighty monolith learning about the Aboriginal Dreamtime, and spent several nights camping out in a swag.

Back in the UK, if someone had asked me to give up a long weekend in the comfort of my own bed, to travel miles into the middle of nowhere to see a big rock and risk being bitten by a number of deadly creatures while I slept, I would have quickly told them where to go. But here I didn't even question it – in fact I initiated the quest. Here it was a rite of passage for every backpacker worth their salt, a must-have tick on the list of 'Things to do before you leave Australia' along with skydiving, getting drunk in Cairns and attempting to surf on Bondi Beach. Everyone did it. So after finishing my job in Sydney towards the end of my working holiday visa, I hit the internet to find a company who would give me the best experience at the big hulk of rock I knew I needed to clap my eyes on.

It was incredible just how many ways there were to 'do' this Australian landmark – by hot-air balloon, camel, motorbike, over one day or a week, staying in a luxury hotel or... the cheapest option, and therefore the most popular among travellers in my situation, a camp under the stars. It was decided: alfresco sleeping was on the cards.

I'll never forget my first night under swag. When the chirpy Aussie guide handed it to me on picking me up from Alice Springs, I looked at him concerned. A swag is basically a complete sleeping mat, bag and pillow wrapped up in a flimsy bug-shield-come-bivvy-bag. I failed to understand how a thin sheet of fabric would protect me from all the nasties lurking. In Australia, practically everything can kill you – from deadly spiders in the city, to Great White sharks in the sea, freshwater crocs in the billabongs and venomous snakes in the desert – and paranoia soon sets in, you believe that they are actively seeking you out. Rather than offering me protection, it seemed more like a convenient way of packaging me up like a giant snack.

But from the moment I saw the sun slump down in the dusky sky, casting a light show of oranges and browns over that giant rock, I forgot all my fears. Gone were my worries about brown snakes (lethal), funnel-web spiders (can kill you in less than two hours) and bull ants (can cause death in twenty bites). Instead, I lay in my fabric cocoon with a piece of bug-shielding net over my face and looked at the stars overhead illuminating the Red Centre with their twinkling glow. The only thing going through my head was 'Wow!' After a blissful night surrounded by the natural world, I felt exhilarated and was thirsty for more.

On my way back from Oz, I detoured to Jordan and headed off into the desert plains of Wadi Rum with a group of Bedouin – the nomadic tribe who call this landscape home. There, I spent days exploring ancient, weathered sandstone *jebels* (mountains), clambering up and over wind-scoured natural arches that link one range to another and sleeping underneath the Milky Way on the lip of a rocky overhang with nothing but a blanket to keep me from the lizards. Despite the apparent dangers hiding behind each stone, all I could do was gawp in wonder at such a wild place.

My last stop before returning to the UK was Lapland – the Finnish part of it, over 200 miles above the Arctic Circle. I had gone from extreme heat to punishing cold, from sleeping on rocky promontories to a heated wigwam in temperatures of –34°C outside. By day, I travelled by husky sleigh or snowmobile, and by night I slept under reindeer skin, peeking out from the canvas doors to watch the night sky. It wasn't the cold that got the adrenaline pumping through my veins – it was the aurora borealis (Northern Lights) coming out to play.

When I finally landed back in Blighty I felt the post-travel blues familiar to any travellers who return home. I'd had some pretty remarkable experiences and seen amazing sights, and for a while, it seemed like the milky grey skies of Britain could never compete. I mooched around the house like a sulking teenager, bemoaning the lack of excitement in my hometown. I spoke with all the cockiness of a backpacker who has read Alex Garland's *The Beach*, and claims to have seen it all. Worst of all, I was completely broke, so any chance of taking off again to any of the exotic places that were filling my wish list was completely out of the question.

Then a few months down the line I was sitting in a bar in Manchester mouthing off about how brilliant it was when I was Down Under. I was in mid-flow with a girl from Wigan telling her about the greatness of Tasmania's Bicheno National Park, when she interrupted me to point out that if a shining lake, trees and fells were what I wanted, then I should head a couple of hours up the M6 to the Lake District National Park. Like a sudden bolt of lightning I remembered the argument I'd had back in Woolloomooloo; I had become the cocksure Australian that I hated so much. I was so wrapped up in the virtues of 'abroad' that I'd forgotten what lay on my own doorstep. I made a resolution there and then to stop being such a tremendous arse and become a tourist in my own backyard.

The very next weekend I stayed with my dad in Wales and got up early to go walking. It was nothing too technical – a brief foray of about 10 kilometres around a local reservoir, a place I'd visited many times as a child. But before that day, I don't believe I had ever really seen the place. The sun was picking out the ripples on the water's surface transforming the large grey puddle from my childhood memories into a glittering pool of possibilities. Interpretation boards I would never have read in the past, I now pored over with intent, hoping to learn more about this landscape that was, all at once, new to me again. The inscribed local legend of a Fairy Freckled Cow had me mentally transforming distant hills into bovine shapes as my eyes searched the horizon, now spotting the intriguing remains of old follies and sheep pens. A climb up a steady slope took me to something of a promontory from where I could hear the 'go back' calls of the grouse hiding in the heather-clad slopes at my feet. It was as if this small unassuming hill was alive and shaking as these nervous birds darted around me. A weaving track led me through a beautiful avenue of twisted trees, then deposited me at something of a shoreline and a little wild beach where I sat for a good while surveying the scene. It was funny how rediscovering somewhere I'd been to many times before as a child, was now, as an adult, like going there for the very first time. And I was loving it.

As I walked the last couple of miles, I passed the ruins of an old homestead where the local farmers who had called this area home, would have spent evenings laughing, storytelling and singing to the sounds of wood crackling on the open fire, the smell of stew lingering in the air, and the familiar sounds of friends enjoying each other's company. The history of the people who lived on this high moorland pre-dated anything I had read about in post-colonial Australia, yet it had never interested me before. Now I couldn't get enough of it – I was like a woman obsessed. Twice I stopped to check out some odd, orange-speckled fungi and three times I walked back on myself to discover new perspectives on the Bronze Age burial ground to my right. I never thought of myself as a history buff, but the fact that there was so much to see and learn about in such a few short miles, really captured my imagination and began to fill a gap that the end of my official 'travelling' had left. I was hooked and remarkably the whole thing had cost me very little in terms of money.

From small beginnings I started to head much further afield, venturing off the well-signposted tracks only occasionally at first, until I was happily climbing mountains and skirting lakes around the country unconcerned whether or not there were waymarkers. But I still felt there was something missing. At first I wasn't sure what I was searching for, only that I was searching. Then, after something of an epic day-walk on Snowdon, it hit me. Visiting these places was all well and good, but I needed to take it further. I needed to prolong the thrill of being 'out there'. Up to that point, if I went somewhere at the weekend, I began my day walks at all-singing, all-dancing, facility-laden campsites, so the first step was obvious – switch from luxury pitches to farms with more basic amenities which would encourage me to spend more time out in the wilds, rather than in the tent. But that wasn't enough. Once back in the safety of a site – albeit basic – the sense of adventure lessened somehow. Then a friend suggested I forgo the campsites completely, and make the move from mild to wild camping – making walks last multiple days, staying out, camping free wherever I liked – mountains, countryside or coast. Doing that would remove me from all mod cons; the only bathroom available would be the one I dug myself, the only shower a wet wipe and the only drinking water sourced from a stream and boiled courtesy of a camping stove. The idea intrigued, scared and excited me all at the same time, so I gave it a go with a number of willing volunteers. The first night I could barely sleep with the novelty of it all, of being able to select your own site right in the heart of the mountains, literally in the middle of nowhere. After surviving my first campsite-free night I was thirsty for more and persuaded my friends to come and join me on further wild camps. The rougher it got, the more it felt like a proper adventure; the higher and more precarious the camp became, the more I wanted to push my tent pitches; the longer I could endure sleeping out, the more exhilarated I felt.

I had become officially infatuated with what I called 'extreme sleeping' – a kind of addictive high-adrenaline sport; but rather than being defined by pushing the boundaries of physical activity, my particular pursuit was marked by a distinct lack of it. But it was more than just an overnight buzz I was after, more than just finding ways to push the zzz's to the max. Along the way, I wanted to prove to both myself and the next person that I met in a bar (Aussie or otherwise), that the landscapes and experiences available right here in the UK could rival anything found elsewhere in the world. That although it is only a small island, there are still wild places far away from crowds and phone reception, just waiting for intrepid backpackers to discover. My quest took me from the most southerly point in England right up to the far northerly outposts of Scotland, as I attempted to discover what makes a good bed for the night. Some of the areas I explored were completely new to me, whereas others were favourites I'd been to before and wanted to experience at night when the starlight makes places more magical and brings out another side to their character, one hidden from day trippers. Along the way I learned a lot about camping – not least how to stuff a sleeping bag back into a compression sack in less than thirty seconds and how to make a mean cowboy coffee – but more than that, I learned a lot about myself. For those of you wondering, I can tell you right now that I don't like to wear khaki. I have no interest in dining on the carcass of a dead pigeon and I don't dress head to toe in outdoor brands to do my weekly shop in Tesco. And just to clarify, I don't have a beard. In fact, I'm so far removed from the traditional outdoor stereotype that if you met me in the street you might not suspect I was a wild camping addict at all. But that's what's so great about extreme sleeping – anyone can do it – as I soon discovered.

Every journey has to start somewhere and my voyage, into our wildest landscapes, began with a single camp. This wasn't just any night under canvas. What made this a truly monumental escapade was the fact that, for the first time, I was doing it all by myself...

CHAPTER ONE

GOING SOLO

'What if you get mugged, or attacked, or eaten by a bear?' cried my friend Jane as I packed my car for the journey ahead.

Her suggestion was ridiculous for two reasons. The first is obvious – there are no bears in Wales of any variety – big cats may have been spotted for sure, but certainly no bears. The second, is that if you take a minute to really think about all the crimes that have been reported in the last twenty years involving muggings or kidnappings, not a single one of them happened in the middle of the mountains of Snowdonia where I was heading.

'Put yourself in the shoes of a would-be criminal, lurking in the shadows, hoping to catch an ill-prepared and vulnerable woman unawares,' I said to Jane, as I slammed the boot shut and walked round to the driver's side of the car. 'Would you choose to lurk in the hinterland of mountain country, having to take all the trappings of a wild walk with you – warm clothes, tent, water and cooking utensils – hoping against hope that a lone woman might just, on that same night, be there too?'

'Well... I... er...' she stuttered.

'Or would you perhaps go and linger in an alleyway in a major city on a Saturday night where at least hundreds of said vulnerable and, let's face it, probably drunk women will pass by?'

She looked at me concerned, 'Well I suppose I see what you mean.'

'Exactly. I will be fine,' I replied smugly and shut the door. 'Besides, there are definitely no wild animals roaming the hills of Wales...' I shouted as I drove off.

Despite my assurances, there were still some niggling doubts in my mind. This wasn't the first time I'd encountered hysteria at my suggestion of wild camping alone. I had friends encouraging me to take them along if they promised not to tell anyone that they'd come, just so that they'd 'know I was safe'. Another local man, who understands me well enough to know that should anything happen (such as a twisted ankle or something serious enough to need assistance, but certainly not life-threatening), I would be far too proud to call Mountain Rescue, gave me his number. He insisted I call him if I was in trouble and he would discreetly muster his teammates to help me out (not that there would be any phone reception should the worst happen).

Off I drove, up the ribbon of tarmac that's the motorway to the north, determined to cast aside the naysayers. Then came the thunder: giant claps of it shaking the sky while sheet rain hammered on the bonnet as I joined the M6. This was an ominous start to something that I – and everyone I knew – had misgivings about. Soon the rain was so epic that I couldn't actually tell where the droplets came down and the upward spray from the tyres began. It was a merging of two watery horizons.

'It doesn't mean anything. It. Doesn't. Mean. Anything,' I told myself as a flash of lightning illuminated the logo-plastered trucks swerving into the middle lane to my left. I turned on the radio for a welcome distraction, almost expecting to hear Celine Dion's 'All By Myself' just to punctuate the ludicrous scenario I found myself in. Instead, I was met with an annoyingly chirpy rendition of Rihanna's 'Shut Up and Drive'. And so I drove on singing as loud as you do when you're the only person in the car, beating the drum on my steering wheel, screeching to meet the high notes (of course failing miserably) and singing the guitar solos as though they were words. As I performed both the lead and backing harmonies, head banging, undoubtedly looking like a lunatic to any passing drivers, I didn't care. I was in my own world and didn't have to explain what I was doing to anyone, and that was the freedom I was hoping to experience on my mini-expedition.

As I crossed the border into Wales, the rain began to ease to a light drizzle, dribbling on my windscreen for a while, before stopping entirely. Edging the car towards the official boundary to Snowdonia National Park, I saw grey clouds beginning to make way for blue sky and when I finally parked the car in a lay-by, grabbed my rucksack and started walking, the sun was blazing overhead.

At this early point in a walk, conversation is usually rife as the apprehension of a couple of days out in the hills is disguised with cheery banter. Being friend-free, I thought I'd miss this chit-chat, but I was so distracted by the apparent change in weather that I temporarily forgot about it and just soaked up the perfect conditions and the clarity with which I could see all the Welsh scenery stretching out ahead. It wasn't until I passed a farm, looked to see Snowdon glinting like a rocky diamond over my shoulder and began to comment on it, that it sunk in. My abruptly-halted sentence seemed to echo in the air and disappear. I was definitely alone and for a second, began to lose my nerve. Up until this point, staying out in the hills overnight by myself was not something I'd done, I'd always chosen companionship over solitude. Now, with the acknowledgement that I really had taken the plunge and would be sleeping out in solitary splendour, my earlier conversation with Jane about bears and muggers was suddenly much less humorous and somehow more sinister.

I took a minute to remind myself of my reason for doing this unaccompanied escapade. Finding wilderness in the UK is supposed to be no easy feat. I know this because these days every man and his dog seem to be desperately seeking it elsewhere rather than here. You can't turn on the TV without stumbling across a tale of some hardened adventurer's journey to an unspoilt and unpopulated corner of the globe. Everyone likes to remind you just how crowded our tiny country is and how built-up it's becoming; we bemoan the lack of empty space and long wistfully for something wild. The thing is, it is here – all around us – but we don't even realise it. It's all a case of perspective; a place can seem more remote when you're by yourself, away from the distraction of a companion. Alone, the silence and time for quiet contemplation can make you see things you wouldn't normally notice when entrenched in conversation. But very few people will ever purposefully go out of their way to find that extra dimension to an outdoors adventure. That's what I was hoping to achieve in Wales that weekend.

'Right, this way then I guess,' I said out loud, trying desperately to sound assertive.

I began to climb the slope and was immediately hit by waves of heat. I had decided to walk along a ridgeline that cuts into the sky opposite Snowdon, Wales' highest mountain. It was tall enough to get some amazing views but also was nowhere near as visited as its closer celebrity neighbour. This was key, I figured, when selecting a pitch for wild camping – especially a proper solitary experience. Aside from the obvious necessary water source, the next element you want is remoteness, and the spot I'd selected for my overnight stay was virtually guaranteed to be free of other people.

My rucksack felt heavy on my back as I climbed the first peak to get up high. I still had my 'car legs' on – not quite warmed up enough to have found my walking rhythm and I still didn't feel anywhere near the freedom I experienced belting out bad pop music in the car. Instead, I just felt a bit lonely. At about halfway, sweating profusely to the point where I was kind of glad that I had no companion to see how unfit I was, it hit me. Why was I racing? Who was I trying to impress?

There are definitely two schools of walkers in my experience. One group – I call the Trig Touchers (partly named because of the Ordnance Survey Triangulation Points that they set their sights on, and also because the abbreviation 'TT' reminds me of the TT you see in the names of fast cars, meaning something like Turbo Tank or similarly implying speed) – get something known as 'summit blinkers'. All they can do is see getting to the top as a goal. The walk up and down is just the means to an end. For them, being outdoors is nothing without the glory of reaching the highest point. They want to get from A to B as fast as possible, there's no time to stop for snacks or slow down for a chat with a stranger, and who the hell wants to linger on the top anyway? Just touch it and leave; job's a good 'un.

The second school I call the Mountain Meanderers. For us, getting to the top is all well and good, but really it's the journey that counts so why the rush for the early start? Of course there's time for another coffee before we head out, and let's just linger here for a while to take in the view (secretly catching our breath and trying to look like we know what we're doing while the TTs shoot by).

Everyone knows that if you go out walking with someone from the other school, then something of a battle will commence. Usually it's a couple. Often they are arguing about one going too fast or the other faffing for too long. But always, the TTs will win. If you're a Meanderer like me, you spend most of the day chasing your sportier model uphill, trying to slow their pace by asking inane questions about the vegetation or view just to try to make them stop and (sometimes literally) smell the roses. A word of warning: this tactic rarely works on a TT. You will usually get some kind of brush-off reply like, 'We'll look at the map back at the car' or 'It's just heather, come on'. Granted, there are the rare occasions when they stop and you manage to race to catch them up and surge with the ecstatic feeling of standing next to them, side by side for once – rather than catching the odd glimpse of their Gore-Tex-encased backside. You quickly wipe the sweat from your forehead, mumbling something about the warm weather (even if it's cold) and try to slow your breathing so you don't sound like an asthmatic walrus, when all of a sudden they decide that the break is over and shoot off again like a hyperactive squirrel.

But here, on my own, I was racing my way up to a summit even though there was no TT to catch up with. I could sit if I wanted to, have a ten-minute snooze if the mood took me, and even turn back to the car and give up on the whole thing if I liked. So I took a breather, removed my rucksack and sat on its cushioned contents as though it were my own personal pouffe. I then rooted around for a chocolate bar and ate the whole thing piece by piece, not feeling the least bit of guilt. This was why I had come in the first place: to enjoy this kind of indulgence. The chance to do things as I wanted, without having to answer to any other person.

Fuelled by this minor epiphany (and possibly a sugar high courtesy of a Cadbury Boost bar), I began up the hill once more, taking it as slowly as I liked. Everything felt easier and I began to relax into it, stopping now and again to watch the distant figures on the top of Snowdon looking over to where I was walking – alone.

A crumbling wall near the top of a minor promontory appeared ahead. It seemed I had nearly made it to the summit of this first bump on the ridge and found myself checking the map in disbelief, certain that this must be a subsidiary false summit.

'Hi,' came the voice of another walker, standing by the pile of stones that demarked the highest point.

Walking in the hills is like stepping back in time. It's a phenomenon I believe scientists have been trying to theorise on for at least twenty years, if not more. Go to any high street in any town or city in the UK and start saying 'hello' or 'where've you been today?' to every person you pass and at best you will get a dirty look, and at the very worst, get arrested for harassment. In the twenty-first century we're just not equipped to deal with that level of friendliness and familiarity and instead prefer the impersonal approach whereby if you don't know me, then don't make eye contact. However, this all changes when you are approximately 97.2 metres from the nearest car park or road (OK, I may have made the measurement up but I will wait for it to be disproved by science before retracting it). Suddenly everyone talks to each other and you'll actually get a dirty look if you DON'T deign to respond. Ignoring someone's 'hello' is, out in the mountains, akin in rudeness to walking up to a stranger, standing next to them and farting very loudly. It's just not the done thing. Here people talk. Anything from hello to weather reports to route choice, what make their jacket is, is that cereal bar they're eating very good and, how do you rate the new Scarpa GTX SLs (they're just boots by the way)?

I'm by no means suggesting that in everyday life we start approaching strangers to discuss our days with them (certainly not if you live down south anyway; if you're up north give it a try – it will probably go down pretty well). But there is something incredibly lovely about it when you're in the outdoors. Maybe it's that social barriers have dropped away; maybe it's because some of us are on our own and looking for conversation; or maybe it's just the thrill of being able to get away with doing something slightly taboo, i.e. speaking to strangers. Whatever the reason, it should be celebrated and cherished and long may it continue.

Having said all that, I was in a state of shock at seeing another live, speaking human being up here. You would have thought I'd been by myself for days, not just an hour.

'Hi, how's it going?' I replied shakily, partly glad of a small snippet of conversation, though partly annoyed that my alone time was being usurped by an unexpected encounter. I didn't want it to lessen my 'real solo experience', though in Wales' most-visited National Park, on a day as stunning as this, I suppose a completely people-free walk was almost impossible. It did give me comfort knowing that help was never too far away and perhaps, though I would never have admitted it had someone asked me during my planning stage, that's why I'd come here.

After a brief exchange about how sunny it had become, I perhaps rather rudely turned and began walking along the ridge, heading west. From there, I had a choice: either to follow the nose of the rock, scrambling on the jagged crests and peering dangerously over the sheer crag-faces that dropped away for hundreds of metres on the right, or to take the path on the left that stuck to the innocuous grassy slope and miss out any hands-on fun whatsoever.

While debating just how brave I was feeling, I heard some voices above. Not just one or two, I could hear six, eight, or more, screaming, shouting and swearing. I backed a few steps away from the incline and sure enough, saw a youth group tackling the scramble ahead. Now if there's one thing that will drive anyone to seek solitude, it's the rambunctious screams of a youth group. Though dressed head to toe in the heaviest and most retro, matching outdoor gear that the centre has available, they are however, doing this by coercion, thereby retaining their coolness. You, on the other hand, are here by choice, making you one step beyond tragic. You are the sad, middle manager that thinks you're one of the gang by taking part in Christmas party karaoke with a tie knotted around your head, wailing away to Bon Jovi's 'Living on a Prayer'. Needless to say, the vibe is not good and if you see such a group, the best thing to do is to get away from them as quickly and quietly as possible. You don't want to draw any attention to yourself, tempting them to call 'rambler' to you as you slink away with a face as red as your socks.

I decided to hang back a few minutes while they gained some ground, planning to sneak around them when they inevitably stopped at the top. Sweat began to drip off my forehead even though I was no longer moving; it was a crazy contrast to the thunder and rain earlier that day. When the coast was relatively clear, I started up the rock – if they could scramble, I was certainly going to – and immediately became aware of the weight of my rucksack pulling me back as I tried to heave myself upwards.

A well-meaning friend had told me before I left that while walking alone isn't innately dangerous, taking a fall by yourself has much more dire consequences. At the time, I laughed this off as a harmless bit of scaremongering, but now, peering over the edge of the crags to a whole lot of air and pointy stone below, I began to appreciate what he had said. Still, I had made a commitment to do this and I was not about to give up now. My determined nature kicked up a gear and I carried on up, taking my time while humming, 'Oh, mmm, halfway there, oh, oh living on a prayer...' By the time I reached the end of the scramble I emerged over the rocks to find, as predicted, the cluster of kids lying on the grass in front of me. There I was, alone, sweating, my hair dangling in front of my sunglasses like frayed string, pale legs glowing white in the sunshine and an inane 'hey guys I'm cool' type of smile glued to my face. I'm not sure they knew what to make of me.

'Hippy,' one of them ventured, looking to the others for support.

'Swampy,' tried another and a few giggled under their breath. I braced myself for the next name, trying to muster up an 'I'm glam and a walker' kind of air to my stride – though resembling a more 'I'm knackered and embarrassed' amble.

'David – that's enough!' said their group leader, a lad who looked barely five years older than the kids he was with. He shot me a sympathetic glance, 'Hi, you all right?' he said.

'Great, thanks,' I answered, quickening my pace to escape. 'Lovely weather for it,' I responded, wondering to myself when exactly I had begun to talk like my mother.

Soon their hyperactive squeals were left in the distance and I slowed my pace again, wondering if there would be more people to meet on this, my big solo camp. The bleat of a sheep startled me as I was lost in my thoughts. Two sheep actually, staring at me as I made my way to the stack of rocks on the next rise. They boldly began to approach and as they were obviously feeling playful I decided to indulge myself too and began to run downhill towards them yelling 'mint sauce!' at the top of my voice. They ran too and I laughed at how quickly I'd gone from respectable walker to animal-terrorising imbecile.

As I reached the top of the bump, I could suddenly see the sea. There's something magical about the presence of mountains and ocean – the power of the two in such close proximity. I sat for a while, trying to set the camera up to do some shots on self-timer, but ending up with more than a few of me walking back to check that it had gone off, or squinting my eyes as I tried to see if the indicator light was flashing.

I looked at my watch for what must have been the first time that day and worked out that I had enough time to climb another high point. From where I stood it looked like quite an epic prospect, but I knew that if I reached the top, I would get a good view down to where I planned to pitch my tent, giving me a better idea of the suitability of the terrain, so all in all, it seemed well worth the effort.

The path dipped down steeply to a col (the lowest point of a ridge between two peaks), before starting to climb again. The descent was pretty tricky, especially with the weight of a rucksack filled with camping paraphernalia on my back, so I had to concentrate on where I put my feet. As I reached the bottom I heard a voice cry, 'Hi there. You doing the whole ridge?' I looked up to see a couple with two dogs approaching me.

'Yep, I'm camping,' I replied, gesturing at my humongous bag. The woman regarded me with a peculiar curiosity.

'But there's no campsite near here, I don't think,' she said, looking concerned.

'I know,' I said nonchalantly.

'Didn't you leave your car in the village?' said the man.

'Uh-huh, I think I arrived as you were setting off.'

'We're headed back there now...' she said as more of an offer than a point of fact.

'Cool, see you then,' I mustered as upbeat a tone as possible and headed off before a couple of steps later, turning to add, 'It'll be fine.' I'm not sure if this was for their benefit or mine.

People are very funny about time when it comes to walking. In the mountains, although we're not governed by a nine-to-five working day, people still seem determined to follow a timetable in rigid fashion. So come five or six o'clock, suddenly the adventure must be over, we must all head back to the car and get ready to have tea in the safety of 'the great indoors'. No one seems to know why staying out beyond this hour is so scary, but just pass someone coming off the hills at this time when you're heading up, and you can see the fear in their eyes – the burning question: 'Why are you heading up now? What do you know about this time of day that I don't?'

The answer is obvious. This is the magic hour quite simply because they have made it so. With the scrum to be back indoors, the outdoors suddenly becomes a serene place. With the crowds gone, wildlife begins to rear its head among the grassy hummocks, on the edges of rocks and high above in the thermals. The sun begins to display its natural lightshow, casting playful shadows on the landscape just for you. It's like seeing the mountains at their best in every sense.

Regardless of the time, a scramble still awaited me so I began up the pale line that cut through the rocks ahead. I gained height pretty quickly and now, in the shadow, was finally free from the heat of the sun. My head was itching like mad though and after stopping to scratch it for the fourth time, I took out my first-aid kit to fish for the emergency sachet of suncream I keep in there. The very thought of needing UV protection would have been ludicrous on my drive here through hours of pouring rain, but now I began to wish I had brought extra, as the more I rubbed it into my face, the more it began to sting.

I shrugged it off and continued up to the summit plateau, grateful to find a large rock to sit on. From here I surveyed the scene, looking down the valley below to check that the campsite I'd selected was as good as I'd pictured it to be on the map. A smattering of old mine workings in clusters of pewter stone dotted the landscape. Beyond them, the ground rose and fell, up and over, to a small peak where at its foot, an old reservoir sparkled in the sun.

Pleased with the prospect ahead, I left the summit and headed down the slopes. Usually the final peak of the day is one to linger on and savour, but with a further final destination awaiting – this time a camp spot – I was eager to move fast. Having seen it from above, I felt confident and excitedly bounded down in a half-walk, half-run. I don't know why I was going so quickly, but seeing as I was alone and could do what I wanted, I continued, picking up speed all the time until I slipped. Nothing major, just a well-hidden rock in the grass that saw me land on my bottom – hard. I swore loudly, though with no one to hear, it wasn't quite as good at relieving pain or frustration.

A pungent smell began to creep into my nostrils as I pulled myself up on my feet and continued downhill. The lower I descended the worse it got. Under my boots, the ground was getting boggy and I had visions of slipping into a hidden puddle and being found weeks later marinating in eau de sheep piss, a thought that made me quicken my pace. I passed the miners' buildings that up close revealed themselves to be dilapidated and covered in moss, and I began to have my doubts about this area that had looked so good from above. To get away from the stench and the waterlogged grass I veered uphill. I began to feel like I had stumbled into the Amazon, suddenly surrounded by metre-high bracken in thick pockets, though instead of a machete, all I had at my disposal was a walking pole. Arms aching, flies in my face, I fought my way through. It was humid and hot and after what seemed like an age, I cleared this infernal plantation and emerged onto a wide track. I was nearly there.

'Baaa!' I heard from behind and looked to see a big, white sheep staring at me.

'Hello, little sheep,' I called, already imagining this as the start of a great friendship. I'd feed him scraps of my camping meal; he'd sit beside my tent like a big woolly guard dog, protecting me from any intruders...

'Baa! Baaa! Baaaaaa!' Or not. He began to come towards me – fast. After a few more disgruntled grunts, he put his head down and charged me.

I ran but he was gaining on me. 'But I'm a vegetarian!' I yelled and just as I could feel his breath on the back of my calf, I turned left off the track and ran down a small bank.

'BAAA!' He was staring me out threateningly.

Amongst all the naysayers before this trip was one friend, Brian, who said: 'If you're going to do it alone take some kind of protection – whether a penknife or simply a sizeable stone you can throw just in case.'

While I hadn't heeded his advice before, I was now searching for some kind of hefty rock I could throw in the sheep's direction. There was nothing. But I was in luck. Another sheep emerged and startled it, leaving me enough time in the kerfuffle to make a getaway. It was a good sign – fate, that eternal shepherd, was definitely on my side.

A few more metres of bracken strimming and I found the clearing I wanted, near enough to a water source to get what I needed for cooking, and flat enough to have a good night's sleep. The muffled sound of the stream, hidden by the overgrown foliage, provided a reassuring soundtrack guaranteed to send me off into a deep slumber – that was if I could close my eyes to the views around me. The ridge I'd trodden that day stretched out like a rocky guardian in the distance. Beneath my feet, the green, grassy carpet lay like a padded mattress on the ground. Right above where I would pitch my tent, a pyramidal peak rose upwards, studded with heather and rock, like the biggest, grandest headboard you could ever hope to find. Even if you brought the best interior designers together to create the perfect bedroom, I doubt very much any of them would have come close to Mother Nature's offering here.

Pleased with my find, I got out my brand-new, one-person tent, bought especially for this trip. Usually I use my old, faithful, two-man tunnel design that I split between myself and a willing companion, but for this trip I wanted one that was light enough to carry alone and definitely easy to erect, so I had treated myself to a new model. I emptied out the contents, hopeful that this would be the start of a long and happy relationship with my geodesic, freestanding shelter, and found myself face-to-face with the oddest tent pegs I'd ever seen. Needle-thin hooks were all I could find, and I did check in the bag several times; they were hardly the key ingredient to keeping me secured to the earth in a storm. Weight-wise they may have been a dream, but if this ground had been anything but soft mud, they would have been totally useless (two of them bent completely hitting a concealed stone as I tried to push them into the ground). Shaking this off as a minor design flaw, I began to unfold the fabric and clip together the poles. Immediately the desired shape was obvious and I surprised myself with having the whole thing standing in glorious dome-like fashion within a couple of minutes. Now this may have been a mere camouflage-green shelter to some, but for me, at that minute, it represented endless possibilities for forthcoming adventures and my tummy began tingling as I started inflating the camping mat.

Then I spotted something. Was it a spider? A fly? I couldn't be sure so I picked it up from my mat and watched as it dropped between my fingers and seemingly disappeared. I rummaged around through my sleeping bag, spilling out items from my rucksack as I did, but it was gone. I was too tired to be bothered with it any longer and grabbed my stove to start boiling water for a camping meal and coffee.

As it bubbled and whirred, I walked down to the water's edge and took my seat on a smooth stone on its bank. Everything was completely still. The air glowed with an auburn luminosity as the sun began to sink lower in the sky and I spent several minutes doing nothing at all other than feeling like a very small element of a much grander landscape.

A rattle of metal-on-metal alerted me to the fact that I'd lingered a little too long. The water in my stove was overflowing and I had the tricky mission of turning off the gas through the now gushing waterfall of scalding water. I screamed, cursing like a trucker as I felt the hot liquid on my fingertips. I poured it on my food and waited for the yellowish shapes of dehydrated curry to come to life. A couple of midges landed on my arms and I swatted them away, thanking my lucky stars I wasn't in Scotland – a place where these little biters are legendary for their determination. 'At least in Wales they're tamer,' I muttered to myself, not fully remembering why I thought this to be a fact, but comforted now that I'd said it aloud. Meanwhile a couple more flew in and landed on my nose. I waved them away again, then stirred my meal. I was starving and it smelt good.

'Oh!' I cried as I felt the unmistakable pinch of a midge bite on my elbow. 'You little...'

I moved away, thinking I'd trick them with my sudden absence, convinced that would be the end of it. Then there were more. I spent the next eight minutes attempting to wolf down fly-free mouthfuls of an ever-cooling curry meal while running in zigzag-fashion around a 10-metre-square patch of grass. Every time I got too close to the surrounding bracken, a new cloud of them would fly up and join the chase – I was their version of a fly-through meal and I wasn't sure there was enough of me to go around their growing number.

'Fine then,' I yelled, pleased to be alone as I must have looked like a woman on the verge of mild hysteria. I threw my sachet into my rubbish bag and jumped in to the tent, zipped up the flysheet and watched the swarm of midges gather like a cheering crowd outside it. I methodically checked every wall of the tent and squished any of them I could see immediately – the animal-lover in me had clearly had enough.

I was annoyed, still hungry, and now a prisoner in my own tent.

Midges still guarding the entrance, I made the decision not to venture out again. I didn't have the energy to make my hot drink, couldn't be bothered to tidy away my stove and wasn't even going to consider heading out to brush my teeth. As I changed into a thin set of base layers I felt my legs begin to itch. There was no bite to see and both legs felt hot. My arms started to itch too, then my neck. Then it dawned on me. Sunburn. I'd only had enough suncream to cover my face and had forgotten that the rest of me was naked to the UV light. Uncomfortable, aching, tired and annoyed with myself, I climbed into my sleeping bag – I had even brought a liner to keep me warm, which now seemed ludicrous – and hoped for sleep to find me easily.

I must have drifted off quickly but the sound of footsteps woke me – like a gentle tiptoeing made by someone trying not to be noticed. Who on earth was out there at this time? It was dark and these feet were close to where I lay. All at once, I was wide awake. I listened as whatever it was, slowly circled my tent. I froze in terror, gulped hard and prepared for the sound of the zip being torn open by this stealthy attacker. But all I heard was the sound of digging. I realised with a relieved chuckle that it was just the padded feet of rabbits. I fell asleep again.

Suddenly I awoke to more footsteps, heavier this time. So much for my pre-trip cockiness.

Not wanting to create any noise doing up the other zip, I slid down in my tent to feel around for something I could use as a weapon. Finding only a Spork (a plastic fork-spoon combination), I peeked above the edge of the flysheet.

It was back. Satanic eyes with black slits running down the middle reflected back at me and it took all my willpower to stifle a scream.

'Baaa!' my nemesis sheep cried as I turned off the torch and slid down into my sleeping bag hoping it would go away. Who would have thought I'd have to worry about being stalked by a big woolly Welsh stereotype? It was about the most ridiculous scenario I could imagine. I didn't move a muscle, barely daring to breathe.

As I lay there, its hoofs pounding the ground around my flimsy shelter, I suddenly realised that, in typical camping fashion, I was desperate for a wee.

'It's fine,' I thought to myself, 'I can wait till daylight.' And I lay there with my eyes closed.

Minutes later I opened one eye. It was still dark. Fumbling around with my hand I searched for my phone, eventually locating the switch to turn on the screen. It was only 2.34 a.m. and there was no way I could hold out till the morning.

I resolutely sat up, unzipped the tent door and slid my feet into my boots. I shone my headtorch out there and could see no sign of my fuzzy stalker. Creeping away from the tent as silently as I could, I hid behind some foliage to take care of business. At any moment I expected to receive a bite on the cheeks, the sheep sneaking up on me ninja-style.

Thankfully there was no sheep but I had other problems. Now my legs and arms were really starting to sting, the sunburn beginning to develop properly. I didn't dare check out how bad it was and just crept back to my tent, hoping this was just a case of middle-of-the-night overtiredness. I somehow fell back to sleep, waking up every so often when I turned over and the fabric scratched my frazzled skin.

Finally, sunlight seeped through the green skin of the tent walls signalling that morning had at last come. My skin felt tight and sore and I was so tired that I would have gladly slept for longer even though I now needed to get up – a phenomenon that many campers will attest to. Despite the sunburn sting and the increasing need to eat, a feeling of elation was growing in my belly. I had survived my first solo wild camp – no attackers, no big cats, no bears and no (real) dramas. Now I could enjoy my breakfast, perhaps by that serene patch of water, pack up my camp slowly and calmly and enjoy the rest of the day with a walk to the station from where I could catch a train back to my car.

Nature, it seemed, had other ideas. I got changed in my tent, trying to ignore the fact that I now had a trucker tan on my arms that was practically crimson, and opened the flap. There on the other side was a mizzle of midges and let me tell you, they were hungrier than me.

I waved them away as I got up and grabbed the stove. But if I stood in one place for more than five seconds they were upon me, chewing my skin as if it were made by Wrigley. After running around like a lunatic for several minutes I had no choice but to abandon plans for a laid-back breakfast, forgo the coffee I'd been gasping for and bundle all my kit away while simultaneously doing what can only be described as an insane, midge-wave dance around the grass. When I had finally packed everything away I was exhausted. If it hadn't been for the sheer exhilaration I still felt from surviving my solo night in the wild, I probably would have cried.

I picked my way through more bracken and twisted undergrowth and over boggy ground until I reached the tracings of a little-used path. It was heaven. I don't think anyone has ever been as excited to see a track as I was that day. Away from standing water and head-height foliage, I cast off my rucksack and got out my toothbrush. Cleaning my teeth felt like a real treat and then following that with a cereal bar chaser was akin, I believe, to the feeling one might experience on winning the lottery. An exaggeration?

Maybe, but right there and then, if asked to choose between the two, I would have gone with the cereal bar and teeth cleaning without hesitation.

Now minty fresh and fed and with another sunny day developing above me, I headed east towards the town, several miles and a couple of hills away. The climb uphill passed by in a bit of a haze and my stumble onto the next one felt like I was watching someone else do it. I should have realised then that lack of sleep and sunburn – being topped up by more sun – wasn't a good combination, but why would I be preoccupied with such trifling matter when I was on the verge of running out of water?

It was when I found myself eyeing a black puddle just off the second summit that I realised things were getting a little desperate. 'Don't panic,' I told myself in a voice more calm than I felt, 'look at the map.'

Staring at its brown contours and black squiggles to denote rocks, I struggled to spot anything resembling the friendly and calming blue of water. Then a thin blue line symbolising a stream seemed to emerge, just downhill of where I was. With no closer options I headed in that direction, only to find it virtually dried up. Luckily, a pool of much clearer water sat a few metres from its terminus, so I scooped it up and got out my stove to boil it.

Everything felt a lot more positive now. I knew I wasn't going to die of thirst and I began to think about how good it would feel to complete the planned route and emerge victorious to tell anyone who would listen about my achievement. The whisper of the bubbles mounting inside the pot stirred me from my thoughts and, for some delusional reason, I began to imagine how good the cold water would feel on my throat.

It wasn't cold of course – it was boiling water after all – so all I could do was put it in my bottle and start walking again. I was convinced it would cool as I went, but even by the summit of the final mountain, it was still too hot to drink. As I made my way down the flanks and saw buildings on the outskirts of a town, I was feeling delirious. I began to pass casual day-walkers heading up this local peak and resented them for their full water bottles. I forced down some of my warm liquid and continued on, emerging on the pavement of the main road looking like a woman who had been lost in the wild for months – not a mere thirty-six hours.

I practically ran into the newsagents and proceeded to gulp down two ice-cold cans of Cherry Coke before continuing on towards the train station. At the ice-cream parlour I practically inhaled a two-scoop waffle cone which I swear to this day was the best ice cream I've ever eaten. Finally I got to the ticket office and relieved, requested a single ticket.

'Sorry – no can do, love,' said the woman behind the glass.

'What's that? Why not?' I asked with disbelief at this last hurdle on my journey.

'Train's broken down on the tracks between this and the other station – don't think it will be sorted today.'

If I hadn't been so tired I think I would have had a meltdown. Instead I just laughed hysterically.

'Sherpa bus is running,' she ventured helpfully and, looking a little concerned (if she'd have had a panic button I reckon she'd have been about a centimetre away from pushing it), pointed me in the direction of the bus stop.

By the time the bus came and I was safely deposited back in the village taking the final steps to my car, I believe I must have experienced, at least in some small way, the feeling that Tenzing and Hillary had on returning from the summit of Everest. OK, so being the first humans to set foot on the highest mountain on Earth was perhaps marginally more headline-worthy, but here and now, my achievement felt every bit as epic.

Only one small challenge now stood between me and victory: finding the car keys. After rummaging through my backpack several times and tearing through my rubbish, I suddenly remembered I had sensibly attached them to a clip in the lid of my rucksack. Wiping away the remnants of cold curry sauce from my fingers, I unlocked the door and sat in the car for several minutes not moving, enjoying the feeling of having no rucksack strapped to my back, smiling to myself.

When I worked up the strength to move once more, I reached into the glove compartment to get the spare top I had stashed there so that I might freshen up on my return. As I changed T-shirts, I glanced down at my side and saw something black with blotchy red around it. Squeezing my skin between my fingers, I leaned down for a closer look. Immediately I let go and rested back into my seat. It was a tick – a nasty parasite that burrows its head inside you, considerately injecting anaesthetic so you don't realise, while it feeds on your blood. It can be removed fairly straightforwardly with some tweezers, as long as you do it in one quick pull and don't leave behind any of its mouthpiece (which I would do later). This was the spider-come-fly I thought I had spotted when inflating my sleeping mat, but had then lost amongst my things.

Thanks to this stowaway from the wilderness, it turned out I hadn't really been alone the whole time at all. And the thought of that made me start to laugh uncontrollably for a full seven minutes. While trying to collect myself, I caught sight of my bright-pink face in the windscreen mirror and managed to reduce my guffaws to the odd, crazy chuckle. I may have been more pink when I finished than when I started, but beneath my sunburn, I like to think that some of my glow now came from the pride I felt at having taken this first step into a whole new world of solo wild camping. From here on I reasoned, things could only get better.

CHAPTER TWO

SOUTHERN EXPOSURE

Waves crashed at my feet as I stared out at the sea below. I looked up to see the sun hanging low in the sky. I was standing on the edge of mainland Britain and under my boots was the most southerly place in the country called Lizard Point. The cliffs, untamed by either man or the elements, were wild and crumbling vertically down beneath where I stood. In the dying throes of incandescent light, the sea's surf seemed so incredibly powerful and unapologetically rough – it was beautiful.

The setting sun was a reminder that night was on its way and seeing as I had come here to experience a wild sleep – southern style – I had to act fast if I wanted to scope out a spot that was not only safe, but also hidden from view. Unlike my solo sleep in the mountains of Wales, where I was so high up that no one would notice or really care that I was there, this was a place were camping away from an official site was not usually tolerated and it wasn't uncommon to get moved on by National Trust wardens if you attempted it. So I needed to find a pitch sharpish, in daylight, before I drew attention to myself with the glare of a headtorch.

I did have several elements in my favour. It was off-season and late in the afternoon, and I was just a single, quiet girl on her own, rather than a rowdy group of lads drinking beer from cans. I reasoned that my chances of being discovered and asked to leave were minimal. Still, I didn't want to be too blatant about it, so I intended to recce the place first without the backpack, select a likely spot, then head back into town till it was late enough that I wouldn't be discovered when pitching my tent. It felt properly covert.

Leaving my kit in the car, I turned west, taking the South West Coast Path along the clifftops and past a group of houses. A woman bringing in washing from her garden gave me an odd look. I wondered if she'd sussed me out and hurried past, enjoying the constant roar of the sea in my ear, like the friendly conversation of a faithful companion.

Having grown up on the North Wales coast I have a real affinity with the sea that I can't adequately explain. I can stand and look at it for hours if I'm not disturbed. Now I live away from it most of the time, hemmed in on every side by the outer districts of London, I am always eager to see it. It gives me a warm and comfortable feeling – like visiting an old relative – and on the journey here I had been like an impatient child in the car. After a quick look at the road atlas, I had mistakenly thought the sea was going to be in continuous sight on the drive down, but surprisingly

– barring the exception of the brief glimpse of the estuary at Plymouth – I didn't get a view of it at all. It was a proper build-up if ever there was one. I shot through each of the small villages feeling increasingly excited, the signposts to Cathedral Cove, Kynance Cove and the one indicating Mile End whizzed by. I knew the coast was tantalisingly close, but it still proved to be elusive and even when I reached Lizard Village, there was no hint of water, just lots of 'No Parking' signs and posters advertising local pasties.

I continued south, hopeful that if I kept going in Thelma and Louise style, the sea was bound to appear. The road became narrower now and the hedges higher; it felt like Cornwall was conspiring against visitors to hide away the main attraction that kept them coming. I followed it round twists and turns, passed another two car parks, each emblazoned with 'no overnight stay' motifs. Then finally, a flock of seagulls gave the game away. I turned another corner, went past the little café, the information centre and obligatory gift shop and there it finally was: the end of the UK.

I was surprised to see that the car park there was not only small and fairly devoid of cars, but was also a donation-only affair, which all seemed very reasonable to me. Throwing a couple of quid into the box, I passed the buildings and walked towards the cliff edge. Just beyond my feet, the ground ended. The tide was high and water thrashed against the land, covering, then exposing blackened rocks that were once part of the mainland, but now dwelt on their own out to sea like crunchy croutons in a frothy soup. It was so deliciously wild and the epitome of the word 'rugged', and yet so insanely commercialised with the gift shop just feet away. It seemed funny to think you might need anything tangible to take away with you to memorise this scene. A shell with the word 'Lizard' on it might prove you had a few quid left when you reached the ends of our earth, but would be nothing compared to spending an hour listening to the evocative roar of the waves or inhaling the salty smells of the ocean. That would give you a lifetime of lasting memories... all for free.

Before the sun began to set, I followed the path that led down to the beach – the one section of sand that was still visible along this southern edge at high tide. The scent of seaweed and fish burst into my nostrils reminding me of my proximity to the ocean. I passed the old lifeboat hut. The rocks that litter the seabed have claimed the lives of hundreds – with Snag Rocks, the most southern of those clustered at Lizard Point, being the worst, hence the name. The lifeboat volunteers have helped to save a great many – the new station is now round the coast a little, based at Kilcobben Cove since 1961. Alongside the old launch was a clutter of little wooden boats and crab baskets intertwined with old buoys and the green slimy spoils of the sea. I continued down until I felt the soft sand underneath my boots and walked towards the water, waves chasing me away as I neared it.

It put me in mind of Cape Reinga, the most northerly tip of North Island, New Zealand where the Maori believe that spirits leave the living world to continue their journey on to the underworld. I had thought that was the best place on earth, but now, standing on the cliff top, I realised this easily equalled it. I didn't know whether I truly expected to find the wild here – tucked somewhere between cafés and car parks, but I was eager to sleep so close to the sea.

After I'd torn myself away from the views and passed the suspicious woman in her garden, the path cut down to a place called Pistil Meadow, which I'd read on an information board was where they had buried the 207 victims of a shipwreck that happened back in 1720. I quickly passed through it, deciding that staying there just wouldn't be right. Plus, I didn't fancy contending with disgruntled ghosts as well as wardens.

I climbed up the other side of the meadow, the path becoming increasingly rocky, and moved onwards along the coast scoping out possible spots. To the right of the track far away from the cliff edge it was definitely safe, but somehow camping on the inland side wouldn't feel like I'd really stayed by the coast. I wanted to experience a sleep as close to the sea as possible, to wake up feeling like I was sleeping on the crest of a wave, feel the wind in my hair and the spray coating my tent. Other potential pitches on the seaward side definitely had potential, but while teetering on the edge of the cliffs might be great in daylight, I had visions of me needing the toilet in the middle of the night and stumbling over the edge in a half-awake stupor.

Moving on a little further, the sun now transforming the colourscape to hushed orange tones, I spotted the figure of a lone walker coming towards me. He was a middle-aged man with a bald head that seemed to reflect in the evening light as effectively as the water did below. His rucksack was huge – bigger than the one I had stashed in my car – and before he saw me, I noticed him doing a familiar series of exploratory glances at the pieces of flattened ground either side of the path. I knew instantly that he was engaging in a similar hunt for an overnight spot.

As he got closer, he caught me feeling out the flatness of the ground under the farm wall and came to a realisation that we were in the same boat – though my absence of a rucksack seemed to throw him. His look of understanding immediately changed to that of suspicion – as if perhaps I were an undercover warden out to move him along. We nodded hello to each other and I smiled to myself, happy for him to come to the wrong conclusion if it meant I could secure the best spot for the night. As I continued, the path seemed to divide – some tracks going high and away from the precipice, some cutting low along it, still others disappearing off to where land had once been but had since slipped away.

I decided to try a lower path, hopeful a perfect pitch would reveal itself, though slightly concerned that if there was one, the other walker would have opted for it. As I cut over the grass, it felt soft and spongy beneath my feet like a bouncy, plush carpet. I was half tempted to lie down right there and then, forgoing the need for a sleeping mat and tent – after all, it was a beautiful night and no rain was forecast. But good sense got the better of me as I realised that so close to a massive 30-metre drop, a spongy surface might not be the sign of stable ground, so I quickly moved on.

About ten minutes later I came to a clearing, a huge expanse of grass where the land seemed to slope down towards the edge of the sea in a more gradual fashion. To the right of the path was an inclining meadow, its long grass wet from the briny sea air. However to the left, the grass was short and the terrain seemed to rise up to a lip near the edge, so that if I did roll over in the night, nature and gravity would surely cause me to roll back.

Better yet, a large boulder was firmly wedged in the ground offering shelter from the wind – which was beginning to whip up more violently than I had anticipated – as well as cover from any prying eyes on the village-side of the path. It would also provide a solid barrier to keep me safe from the drops all around me. This would work. This would be the spot where I'd watch the sun rise in all its glory.

Satisfied and smug I walked back in the direction of my car. So sure was I that I'd found the perfect place that I even indulged myself a little by taking a rest on a bench to watch the sun glow yellow and ripple its warm palette on the swell beneath. Fulmars began to swoop and dive above my head, the lights from the homesteads in Lizard began to switch on one by one in the near darkness and I could see the last few headlights leaving the car park. This, I told myself as I walked the final few steps to my vehicle, was going to be perfect.

To kill some time and warm up before my impending night out, I headed to one of the few pubs that I could find open. I sat in the snug, enjoying the warmth that comes not only from being indoors when you know you'll soon be heading back outside, but also from the company of other people busy in their lives around you, who are totally unaware of your secret adventure. They sat discussing neighbours, work colleagues and what time they had to be at the office the next day; whilst I was building up for a step beyond the mundane, planning a wild night out under the stars in a place where, just for those few hours, none of the worries of ordinary life would permeate.

Lost in this feeling I was suddenly jolted out of it by a woman who wanted to know if I would be partaking in the pub quiz. I politely declined – these kinds of things have never been 'my thing' as my general knowledge ranges from bad to shocking, especially in a room full of locals who would clearly fight tooth and nail to defend native honour. It seemed though, that she wasn't willing to give up so easily.

'But you're sitting at that table. That table is reserved for the quiz I believe, so you should be doing the quiz.'

I looked around to try to catch the eye of the bartender, but he was preoccupied watching an amusing conversation between some young lads who were questioning the sexuality of their friend after he dared to ask for lime in his Corona beer. I was stuck.

'Sure, I guess so, I mean...' I trailed off as she began stopping another intruder from sitting down in the quiz ring. She looked back at me warmly, pleased there would be someone for the regulars to beat. Suddenly, despite the warmth and smiles, the promise of a possible dessert and coffee, and the thrill of just one more drink before I left, I wanted to be outside on the coastline again, where I could sit where I liked and not have to answer any questions. I muttered an apology about needing the ladies' room, then headed off sharpish, slipping out of the side door like some kind of fugitive.

The sting of a frosty night hit me immediately, any sleepiness induced by the hot food instantly subsided as I saw my expelled breath materialise in front of me in a veil of cloud. Now the darkness was complete. It would take me a while to walk down to the start of the path, but I felt happier leaving my car here so as not to arouse any suspicion.

I retrieved my backpack, looking about me as I slammed the boot shut and hurried off down to the sea, the hedges thankfully shielding me from the road. Small bats began to appear overhead, flapping past me and plunging up and down in the night air. I could hear insects chirping in the undergrowth and feel the vibrations of rabbits scurrying about near my feet – I prepared myself for a night of hearing odd animal noises.

Then I saw the thing that I had completely forgotten to take into account.

A huge beam of light, more powerful than any torch, swung round to face me before shooting off the other way. Three seconds later it did the same again – and again and again. It was the Lizard lighthouse – the landmark that protects seafaring vessels by alerting them to how close to land they are. The same beam would make camping discreetly a tad more complicated courtesy of my glow-in-the-light-of-a-torchbeam guy lines.

Not that I could blame anyone for putting the lighthouse there. Hundreds of years ago, this stretch of coast was renowned for shipwrecks. The hidden rocks were, and still are, lethal. But it wasn't all bad for the locals. The money they could make from salvage – claiming loot lost at sea when it washed up on the shore and then selling it on – made some of them very rich indeed, to the point where the first lighthouse built in the 1600s was promptly torn down as it was seen as being bad for business. The willingness to preserve life was eventually won in 1752 with the building of another lighthouse, and its great circling beacon casts a beam out for around 40 kilometres, even adding a loud foghorn toot in really bad mist to alert those at sea of the presence of land.

I'd never seen a working lighthouse in the UK before. There was something quite hypnotic about it and I stood for a few minutes watching. Conveniently ignoring the fact that this bright searchlight might spell trouble for my wild camp, I continued on towards the sea. The sound of a musket shot being fired stopped me dead in my tracks, transporting me almost immediately back to a Cornish past when buccaneers worked the shoreline, hiding loot in the caves that lurk below the cliff faces and are only accessible when the tide retreats. Then it sounded again, this time resembling more of a roar of thunder. It wasn't a gun. It wasn't a fluke storm. This was the sound of the sea hitting the rocks below, creating a reverberating crescendo that tore through the darkness.

My heart was beating fast now as I edged onto the coast path and closer to the source of this din. Below, though I couldn't see the water clearly in the dark, I could make out the white frothy tips where the waves crashed onto the shore. Above, stars filled the sky, scattering their little pinprick spots of light across the inky canvas. I swear I'd not so seen so many since I stood in the middle of the desert in Wadi Rum with the Bedouin, gawping at the Milky Way from high on a mountain ledge.

I paid special attention to the path. I was reluctant to put my headtorch on, but even less keen to fall to a sticky end because I'd been too proud to switch it on. I reasoned that the lighthouse beam would suffice and continued cautiously, moving fast under the light and stopping when it swung away. I half expected to see a dog walker at any minute. They are always a nightmare when attempting a less than legal wild camp – cropping up when you least expect it. But now, there was no one else here.

Out to sea was a different story. I was flabbergasted at the sheer volume of traffic making its way west on the waves. Miles out to sea, the little lights from cabins glowed cordially as they bobbed like rubber ducks on the water. I almost felt like I could reach out and pick one up. So taken was I by this sight, imagining where these souls might be heading on their night-time voyage, that I was beginning to draw a bit of a blank as to where my planned sleeping spot was going to be.

Straining my eyes I looked for something familiar, but now each cliff edge looked like the one before it, each boulder as solid as the last, and I was beginning to feel tired. Walking on a little further, my eyelids heavy, I knew there was nothing else for it, I had to bite the bullet and pitch up, even if it wasn't the camp spot I'd lovingly selected earlier.

I needed to choose which side of the path I wanted to go for. The safe but dull inland side, with its comfy long grass; or the edge, complete with gaping drops, rocky lumps, but stunning views. After about nine seconds of deliberation (measured accurately by three spins of the lighthouse beam), I opted for the latter and headed off on one of the lower level paths which skirted nearer the rim, merely metres away from the ocean.

Here I felt hidden enough that a late-night walker might miss me, and just far enough from a drop that I wouldn't accidently slip off while I slept. I took out the tent, and realised that in my haste to leave the town unnoticed, I had failed to substitute my large, oversize, comfort-first tent – ideal for the less controversial wild camps – for the small bivvy bag more suited to this kind of covert camping mission. It was too late. I just had to get on with it. I began snapping the poles together. The tent might have been big, but it was also light and a sudden gust nearly took it over the brink. I grabbed it and fought to secure the other poles. The inner skin was erected but every three seconds its bright yellow seemed luminous in the lighthouse beam. I needed to get the dark green outer sheet on – and fast. Using my feet to weigh it down as the wind tried to wrestle it away from me, I flung it over the skeletal frame and instantly it blended into the night. With pegs in hand I ran around securing it to the ground, corners first. Some of the pegs went in easily, others were harder, hitting stones and consolidated muddy ground, steadfastly refusing to go any further.

The wind was violently flapping the fabric about and I dug around in the bag for extra pegs to help secure it. Normally I'd try to help weigh the tent down with boots or items of kit on the outside, but I was scared I might lose them if the gusts became any stronger and decided that it was safer just to clamber in and use my body weight to anchor my little home. With one last glance before I zipped up the entrance, I convinced myself that no one from the houses on the edge of the village would be able to see me here, and crawled inside. Even though I've been doing this camping malarkey for a while now and know what to expect, when you are inside a small tent in strong wind, it can still be shocking how noisy it is.

The fabric was beating violently and didn't show any signs of relenting. I unfurled my sleeping bag and climbed inside, hoping that my weight would keep everything grounded – which of course given the dinner I'd just ingested should have easily been the case, though perhaps I should have had dessert. The roof kept bouncing down almost to my nose before pinging back up with a happy 'whoop' sort of sound, as if a rabbit was trampolining on my tent. As long as it kept bouncing back up I was content, but sleeping against all the noise was proving to be a problem.

On top of the wind, which whistled relentlessly, was the sound of the sea itself. The noise was at times deafening, rumbling like the roar of machines in a quarry – crashing and banging with a forcefulness that made me shiver and then minutes later, dying down to a gentle and absorbing lull. I felt like one of the adventurers I'd seen on video battling the extremes of an Antarctic crossing. Everything shook around me, from the land under my body to the sky above my head. This felt surprisingly epic for a place so close to the boutique hotels with their doilies and chintzy furnishings. I was pleasantly surprised. When in the 'proper' wilds of mountainous Wales, the silence had, at times, been deafening, every soft sound and rabbit foot amplified by the stillness; here it was like being in a nightclub, with strobe disco lighting from the lighthouse illuminating my tent guy lines every few seconds. The sound was on a par with having a heavy metal band thrashing away outside and the wind flapping around like old-fashioned wooden clappers at a football match. And yet, despite this incessant racket, clattering and clamouring, each sound louder than the next, I fell asleep remarkably quickly – their white noise drowning out any wildlife noises or walkers' footsteps that I might have otherwise heard.

It was the morning caterwauling from seagulls that startled me. The sounds of the sea had died down to more of a purr rather than the hullabaloo and commotion of the night-time. Although a natural noise, after laying there for several minutes I confess I found myself wishing there was a way to silence the blasted birds. At first I thought the light I could see coming in through the tent walls was still from the lighthouse, but as I lay there, it dawned on me that it was too consistent to be that and the seagulls seemed to be calling 'Late! Late! Late!' The alarm I'd set to enable me to rise before anyone was up had been lost, its cheery beeps swallowed up by the din outside. I picked up my phone to see the time – it was already nearly 9 a.m. – so much for wild camp etiquette where you always aim to be packed and away before anyone can see you.

I hurriedly grabbed my top and struggled to unzip my sleeping bag. Sure enough, when I did pull myself outside it was well and truly sunup and – to my utter horror – I had perched my tent on a prime piece of coastal real estate in clear view of anyone whose house looked out that way. And now, though clearly about 2 kilometres along the path, I could just about make out the figure of a walker – I needed to move fast.

I shoved my belongings into my rucksack, desperately trying to deflate my sleeping mat while sitting on my compression sack at the same time as squeezing the extra air and space out of my sleeping bag. Coming across my stove I put it on the floor outside my tent – if I was going to be caught and chastised I was damn well sure I would do it with a hot coffee in my hand. Then I set about unhooking the tent fabric from the poles. The sea may have been on a temporary calm, but the wind had not yielded and as soon as I began to remove the pegs, the tent cover tried to escape me again. I sprawled myself over it, draping arms and legs in strategic ways to weigh it down as I unclipped the flysheet and screamed as it engulfed me in its swathes. Spitting out the material I began shoving everything into the stuff sack whilst clasping the peg bag in my teeth. I was dogged in my determination to get this tent packed away before the walker reached me. As I got the last of the fabric unhooked, one of the poles flew off up the cliffs. Thankfully its metallic blue was easy to spot and seconds later, I had it as well as the rest of the fabric and pegs safely stowed away in my bag. I filled my stove with water from my bottle and began heating it up, my mug and a piece of brioche laid out beside it for breakfast – to the unassuming eye I looked like a picture of tranquillity and calm. When the walker strolled past me I smiled and he nodded back, looking envious at my spread. I kept up my charade while he walked past and then, when he was far enough away not to hear me, let out my breath with an all-encompassing sigh of relief.

Feeling like a true success story, I drank my coffee with pride and finally took my time to appreciate the great surrounds. The sea was beginning to pick up with roller after roller breaking against the land, spray shooting up to almost the same height that I was standing. Though windy, the sky was now bright and alive with early morning colours, highlighting the groves and fissures in the clouds. This was too good a scene to miss.

Putting away my stove, I continued a little further on down the path. To my absolute delight things seemed to become wilder the further I went. The rocks appeared more blackened and wave-worn. The grass seemed less pristine and the path became a mix of track and stone. Out towards the sea, another path that led down to the beach had been closed off and warning signs posted. At first I thought it was just a classic case of Health and Safety gone mad, then I gained some height. Looking down I could see a flight of steps vanish where the cliffs had crumbled away into the water below. It was like looking at an Escher etching, all these paths leading off into nowhere, the land a jumbled jigsaw of man-made mounds and natural troughs. I took a couple of steps further back from the edge. Never could anyone accuse the southern areas of being a soft touch. This landscape meant business.

A little further on, I emerged into a gorge that offered some shelter from the wind where a bunch of Shetland ponies had gathered together higher up the slopes. A sign explained their ability to cling onto uneven terrain with ease and survive in harsh conditions. The ponies had clearly decided to ignore the sign and were staying well away from any crags, keeping their hoofs on the softer grass.

Kynance Cove was my goal. I was keen to see its impressive assemblage of wave-beaten rocky protrusions. They had once belonged to the mainland but were now broken off and left out in the water, continuously scoured by tides. A toll road brings most visitors to it, but arriving on foot is so much more rewarding. After pacing fairly even ground for a while, I reached the best viewpoint. A lookout spot allowed me to gaze down onto the headland, whose weather-worn bay was festooned with a cluster of white stone houses and the practically obligatory café for day trippers. Off the mainland, dark slices of rock jutted out from the water near the shoreline while larger, slabby wedges of grass-covered lumps bulged above the waves further out to sea. These fragments of land, and the crumbled steps that led to nowhere before, were testament to just how strong this sea could be. If stone that is millions of years old is no match for the sea's power, then man-made structures that try to harness safe access for tourists certainly aren't either. The waves are so unashamedly powerful and commanding, no matter what controls we try to impose, they will eventually choose where they want to go; whatever lies in their path will soon lie on the ocean floor.

Smiling at this thought, where the landscape again chooses its own destiny, I started to head back. Rain had begun to fall and the sky was threatening storms on the horizon. Retracing my steps I spotted places where a small bivvy would tuck in nicely and promised myself a return visit with a less extravagant tent.

CHAPTER THREE

DARTMOOR

On arriving at Ivybridge I had, for some odd reason, a rare hankering for chips – proper chippy chips, covered in grease, wrapped in a buttery piece of bread. So strong was this urge, that I delayed heading up to the moorland I had come to seek out for my next wild camp and approached a local to find out if there was somewhere nearby. As I began to ask my question, I could see him smirking. Just as I was starting to think how much his accent sounded like the kind of impression you do of a farmer when you're a child, I realised he was clearly amused by my voice, going by the look on his face. He looked bemused as he glanced down at my walking boots and up again at my softshell jacket. This clearly wasn't a community used to seeing walkers stumble in late at night dressed like Rachel the Rambler. He had to fight to gain composure as he answered.

Unperturbed I went into the fish and chip shop and ordered my chip butty – a phrase that must of course be adapted depending where you find yourself – from buns and baps, to barms, batches, teacakes and muffins (of which the last two I swear are actually different baked goods in their own right and nothing at all to do with what you make a sandwich out of).

'Do you mean a burger bun?' sniggered the girl as she totalled up an inflated price for what she clearly thought was an outlandish request and passed me my order number. I stood with the others and started to wish I hadn't bothered. I was eager to be out of the town and up on that high moorland whose looming shape I'd been able to make out from the road, despite the fact it was already dark. At once my order was called and the same girl who'd served me seconds earlier refused to give it to me without my ticket, as if I was the kind of troublemaker who steals other people's chips. For her it seemed my outdoor attire equated me with someone down on their luck. After finding the ticket crumpled up in my pocket, I left with slightly cooler chips and an annoyed rhythm to my steps.

I was glad to leave the town that, though small, seemed all at once too busy for me. Looking at the map I spotted an access point to the main Two Moors Way, a bridleway that cuts through the moors above Ivybridge. It seemed a great way to get high up and less than 2 kilometres of walking on a footpath from the nearby hamlet of Hartford would deliver me onto it straightaway, so I headed there.

Following the road up through the housing estates, it suddenly plunged me into high-hedged narrow roads that seemed to be getting ever tighter around the car. The tiny distance it appeared on the road atlas didn't seem to correspond with the amount of time it was taking me in reality. I swung to the left, then the right, dipped down to a low point in a thick clump of woods then began to climb up again – as I was starting to wonder if this self-inflicted roller coaster ride would ever end, I saw a stone cross ahead, then behind it a church tower – I knew this was my destination.

I pulled into a small parking area in what looked like the village centre, wanting to leave the car in some form of civilisation rather than abandoning it in the car park slightly further up the road behind a farmer's gate. I wolfed down my chips, which by now had lost all their appeal, and hurriedly counted some coffee sachets and cereal bars into my rucksack. Finally, a little before 10 p.m. I headed off on foot.

Of all the places I could think of in southern England, Dartmoor was the obvious one to head to in search of an extreme sleep. This was mainly because outside of Scotland, it is the only area in Britain where you can legally wild camp – meaning one level of worry is removed from the whole experience, a welcome relief after Cornwall. But I'd always been put off by Dartmoor before as it always seemed, from descriptions I'd read, pretty featureless and flat. It was nice that they were open-minded enough to encourage responsible campers to pitch where they liked, but in a way that almost made it seem even less exciting. Until I learned about the Big Cats.

Since 1976, when the Dangerous Wild Animals Act came into force making it illegal to keep wild animals as pets, there has been a flurry of sightings in the UK's wild spaces of every type of fierce feline – from panther to leopard, lynx to puma and all the other species in between. In 2011 alone, there were fourteen different reports of a black cat nicknamed the Beast of Dartmoor in this National Park. Not that it's a new idea. For centuries, folklore had a spectral black dog roaming out in the moorland, inspiring the Sherlock Holmes story, *The Hound of the Baskervilles*, set on the actual moors where I was going to sleep. I was intrigued. The thought that this might turn into a kind of safari trip added an extra dimension to an otherwise bog-standard wild camp.

With the tarmac road under my boots, I passed the familiarity of houses, their lights glowing at the curtained windows giving a safe orb of comfort, and continued uphill through trees. The branches curved over the way ahead in that *Sleepy Hollow* kind of Tim Burton horror film style – perfect scene setters for spooky happenings. The hedges were moving either side of me with the life of the night dwellers that lurked inside. I began to pant for breath and realised that without knowing it or meaning to, I had quickened my pace to something not far off a light jog. I forced myself to slow down. I still had a fair way to go and didn't want to waste all my energy in the first five minutes before I'd even reached the moors. Overhead an owl hooted. 'You've got to be kidding me,' I almost said out loud. Never in my life had

I heard one so note perfect – it sounded like a sound bite from a Hammer horror film.

The shine of my headlight bounced back at me as it hit the metallic sheen of the gate to the official car park and entry to the moor itself. I opened it up, trying hard to look for signs of life as it screeched and creaked. Three white blotches stopped and six sets of eyes stared at me – sheep – startled apparently by this strange human who had so rudely shattered their night-time revelry. They seemed to have been made twitchy by my presence and I wondered if they knew about the four-legged predators that were supposed to prowl this moorland too. Shaking that thought from my head for the time being, I surveyed the surrounds to try to work out my best course of action for finding a camp.

A single bridleway sign pointed off to my left towards a wall and a solitary car sat in the car park. I hoped for a fleeting moment that the occupant wasn't a weird lunatic out on the hunt for innocent wild campers. A conversation I'd had with my friend Mandy came back to me – not dissimilar to the one I'd had with Jane at the start of all this – in which she had said, 'I hope you don't see any murderers up there.' I had laughed it off again with the carefree retort 'there's no such thing as moors murderers' as I put down the phone and then the horrible realisation sank in that the exception to that rule was of course THE Moors Murderers.

Either way I was here now, I was committed and I'd be damned if I was going to have eaten a huge portion of greasy chips without walking them off. So my desire to stay trim, rather than my worry about being murdered, was what made me keep on target with my trek that night. Plus I decided, if a big cat was lurking about, he was bound to take down a nasty roaming killer rather than a vegetarian asleep in her tent (or at least I hoped that would be the case).

As I emerged from under the shadow of the trees, the darkness became somewhat brighter. I looked back and could see the lights from Ivybridge comfortably dazzling below and felt instantly better. Civilization was there – at a distance, but definitely within reach. Above, a whole blanket of stars shone brightly while the moon smouldered under a passing cloud, peeking out every so often to help light the way. Any misgivings instantly evaporated; I was happy to be here rather than there. Even the occasional darting birds that without warning launched themselves out of the gorse either side of me were no longer making me jump, more fight to get a glimpse of what they might be before I lost them to the night.

Underfoot, though I couldn't really see it properly, I knew that the path was becoming increasingly muddy and you couldn't tell if the surface was going to be solid or sink and suck at your ankles. Yet striding with a purpose, I felt a growing confidence. I should have been timing myself; I should have been pacing to know when I'd reached my path. It occurred to me that it was anyone's guess as to how long I'd been walking, yet I still had a real sense that everything would somehow be all right.

I was on the lookout for a crossroad of paths, where the loosely cut one I was treading on would intersect with a much more established track coming in from the right and left. I also knew that at that point, the path I was currently on would begin to veer downhill, so despite the dark I would be aware if I began losing height and I could use this as a backup method to know that I was in the right place. Right now I could feel, even though I couldn't really see, that my route was still heading uphill and this was all the reassurance I needed to get me up there.

It struck me how much more confidence I had after just two solo wild sleeps. Walking in the dark, I had already devised a strategy for confirming my whereabouts and I felt a shot of warm pride inside my belly. Busy congratulating myself, it was a strange feeling in my feet that indicated that something had changed. The ground had firmed up in a big way. Instead of squishy mud, it was a solid surface strewn with gravel. It had to be the Two Moors Way bridleway. It was so well defined it looked not unlike a country road that had merely been left for a few decades without maintenance. Being on Dartmoor I didn't have to worry about being as discreet as I normally would, as now I had reached this height – well away from people's houses and homesteads – I could simply bed down wherever I fancied. I looked at the map; there was supposed to be a summit of sorts up ahead, just off the main path – though in truth it would be hard to find in the dark – only about 20 or 30 metres higher than the ground I now stood on. With no other options immediately springing to mind I turned north on the path and began walking away from the town.

There was nothing around for miles and miles in front of me. The darkness stretched on endlessly; the lights from the towns and villages nearby had vanished from view. In the beam of my headtorch and just at my feet, a little dormouse was jumping and running a few footsteps ahead. Every few seconds it would pause for breath and look back at me, to see if I was giving chase, then soldier on again trying to escape. It was comforting in an odd sense, like having a little companion. We continued together for quite some time till it got sick of the chase, seized a moment when I paused to look at the map, and darted off to the side of the path where it disappeared into the grass, which was getting increasingly taller.

With my visual entertainment gone, I went back to scanning either side of the path to see if there was anything resembling a summit on the horizon. There was nothing in the immediate vicinity, but a few steps later I saw a rise to the right, almost a mini hill. I stopped. I ran my headtorch beam from one side to the other, it was the only rise within the current area.

Leaving the path, I climbed the few steps to the top and once up there felt somehow safe and knew this should be the place to call home for the night. With the lights from the town only a distant flicker, I pitched the tent.

I still had with me my more generous sturdy model that I'd used on The Lizard (in fact it could take two people at a push). As I didn't have to worry about being too discreet (unlike by the sea), it seemed to be the perfect choice. I had chosen the tent as it wasn't much heavier than a regular one-person model and the colour-coded poles and clips made it much easier to pitch – meaning I could have it standing within minutes. Once inside, I could fit my rucksack in with me – a real sign of a generously proportioned tent. I unpacked and arranged my kit, luxuriating in the fact I could take my time with no high winds to battle and no lighthouse beam to dodge.

In a way, there isn't a great deal of difference between camping in a proper campsite and doing it wild. Aside from the obvious lack of facilities, the experience can be pretty similar – especially in a place like Dartmoor where it's 100 per cent legal so there's no concern about getting into trouble. Yet there is still a definite line drawn between people who will do it and people who won't. Even in a place like Dartmoor, some folks are still worried about staying out in a place that doesn't have official pitches and lines drawn up with designated arrival and departure times – it's as if the freedom scares them.

Thinking about this I couldn't help but remember a woman I met a little while ago called Marion Shoard. She's not a household name, but she should be. In the 1970s she got annoyed when she found out that a little patch of wilderness close to where she lived in southern England, was private land. She longed to explore it, to find out what it was like to stroll under its canopy of trees – but access was denied. She could even see it on her Ordnance Survey map of the area, which further heightened her desire to walk there. The fact that an individual could deny someone the ability to explore a landscape fuelled her passion to campaign for walkers' rights. She penned several books with impassionate and emotive titles like *This Land is Our Land* and *The Theft of Our Countryside* in which she undertook swathes of research to prove why we should all have the right to roam. The research was key to the passing of the 2000 Countryside Rights of Way Act in England and Wales that gives us all the right to explore designated 'Access Land'. When I met her, despite the fact that she was in her sixties she was still getting involved whenever she saw walkers' rights threatened – such as the Government's recent plans to sell off our forests. I'd been inspired after our encounter to make a point of walking away from paths when I could to try to discover more wild places within our country. I can't help think that it was her encouragement to push boundaries that spurred me on to seek out and embrace some of the less legal camps to prove that it could be done responsibly.

Part of the problem, I mused as I sipped my freshly-brewed hot chocolate and surveyed the rolling moors around me, is that when some people hear the term 'wild camping' they immediately picture gaggles of unruly teenagers drinking cider and using the outdoors as a place to get away from their parents. This may be a stereotype, but it is the reason that so many places forbid it. Perhaps if it were legal in more places like Dartmoor, children could be shown how do it properly while they are younger, which would make them more respectful wild campers when they get older. Everyone would know what to do to have minimal impact on the environment, and by being out in it more, they would develop a love for the wild spaces and actually want to make their own efforts to protect them. I confess that I too had been worried that because wild camping is legal on Dartmoor, I was going to be faced with a scene not dissimilar to the fields of Glastonbury festival, with bunches of campers turning the moors into an informal gathering place, littering the landscape with discarded food wrappers and toilet paper. Looking about me now, at the empty silent space, I knew that I had been worrying unnecessarily. If Dartmoor proves anything, it's that legal wild camping is actually the cure to people ruining the landscape, not the cause of it.

On that thought I glanced down at my phone to see that it was now well on the way to midnight. I still felt full from my chips and decided to clean my teeth and visit the 'bathroom' before turning in. I closed my eyes tightly for a few seconds then switched off my headtorch in an attempt to gain my night vision more quickly. Stepping outside, I immediately froze. I could now make out a bigger rise much further away in the distance – this was the tor that I would have come over if I had followed the bridleway from the centre of Ivybridge; now there seemed to be a light moving around on it – a person?

Remembering with a mild panic my earlier thought of moors murderers, I instinctively crouched down, hoping that I would be harder to spot, though knowing from previous experience with a certain lighthouse that the guy lines on the tent would light up like a Christmas tree should this walker shine their headtorch in my direction. There I sat for several minutes watching the light. It was bobbing around sporadically; it looked like a walker was coming up from the town side of the hill and it would only be a matter of time before they reached the summit. It seemed an odd time for a walk, but then who was I to judge I thought, as I sat and waited.

Several minutes later and the fresh breeze of the midnight air was beginning to chill me all over. I grabbed my insulated jacket from the tent and immediately felt my torso warming up. I pulled the hood up over my head and sat staring ahead at the moving light once more. The light was awfully bright and kept shooting round from both sides of the peak. It was taking an inordinately long time for whoever it was to summit. I grabbed the map and started working it out in my head. Even at a slow speed, whoever was coming should be at the top by now. I couldn't understand it.

I took a minute to concentrate on what was happening. The movement was actually quite a smooth flow rather than the jerkiness that comes from the light of a tired walker moving uphill. Perhaps it wasn't a person after all? It went away for a while, and then started again – a smooth movement from one side of the slopes to the other. I took another look at the map – then it was obvious – and I felt stupid, not believing how naive I'd been. The main road ran behind that tor. The lights I could see were not from a headtorch after all, but actually the passing beams of headlights from the steady stream of cars on the A38 below as they passed in front of the hill.

Now reassured that I was quite alone, and with a final glance around the landscape, I headed back into the cocoon-like warmth of my tent, feeling sleepy. I lay there for a while, slowly warming up again and enjoying the squishy sensation under my back that was my inflatable sleeping mat. Within minutes I had nodded off.

A munching sound woke me up, quite rudely at around 3 a.m. and I knew instantly that it was a rabbit chewing on the grass around my tent. I turned over and realised just how cold my back was from facing the outside wall. My nose was like an ice cube too so I lifted my hand to cover it temporarily – it was so cold it stung. Waking up in the middle of the night in a cold tent is often quite disorientating. Getting back to sleep should be just as if you were home – you realise the time, simply turn over and you're off to sleep again; in a tent, it's not always that easy. For a start when it's cold, you are suddenly aware that parts of you are going numb, which can make going back to sleep tricky. It was also very quiet. The quietest of all the extreme sleeps I'd done so far. Silence is, of course, recognised as being conducive to a good night's sleep, but here it was eerily quiet, I was very aware of my own breathing and when I moved, the rustle of my sleeping bag seemed to fill the air around me. The silence itself seemed loud, deafening almost. It was the mirror opposite of the night by the sea where nothing was audible through the din; all sounds were stolen by the wind and the waves. Yet now even the lightest breeze that flapped the outer sheet of my tent just a little, sounded like the footsteps of a runner pounding along the tracks.

Keen to enjoy these extreme sleeping experiences rather than merely endure them, I decided to nip my nerves in the bud straightaway. I sat up in my tent and rubbed my eyes. Right now, my imagination was getting the better of me. Those big cat sightings I'd read about pre-trip and all the associated footage and blurry photos of what had been compared to even a wolverine and other alpha predators, were running through my head. Suddenly, I inexplicably remembered *The Ghost and the Darkness*, a film about lions attacking railway workers in India and began to feel a little like a sitting duck, wrapped nicely in a canvas package.

Fully awake now, I listened to the silence to see if I was imagining things or not. This time though I was certain I could hear something moving around on the ground next to me. I held my breath, it sounded so loud. Then came a loud 'muuooo' followed by some clumping steps and the sound of munching grass. It was a cow. I let out my breath in a huge sigh of relief.

I unzipped my sleeping bag and poked my head outside the tent flap to survey the scene to see if there actually were any leopards or lynx, because surely if there were, the chance to sneak up on a prime piece of steak would be too great to resist. I pulled on my hat and gloves and tucked my base layer pants into my socks to keep me warm, and then wiggled further out to take a proper look.

The cow seemed unconcerned by my presence as it pulled another clump of undergrowth from the ground and chewed nonchalantly. Looking ahead there were no lights coming from the road beyond the moors now, it being either too late or too early, for people to be out. There wasn't enough light to see all that well into the landscape but I could hear the movement of other cattle further away from me, each one of them unconcerned with my presence, all of them blissfully unaware of the apparent danger of being devoured by a big cat.

A while ago, I'd been to Rannoch Moor in Scotland, a place much like Dartmoor in character – high moorland, fairly inhospitable in bad weather due to its rather featureless terrain that makes navigation difficult, and bogs scattered across its grassy landscape in great number. In a lot of ways, environments like these can be more dangerous than the high mountains. At least there you know about the dangers – you're aware of your height, the consequences of a fall and the sharpness of the rocks. But these lower, less immediately obvious wild places, have less apparent hazards. I moved my eyes slowly around the moorland, stopping whenever I saw something that looked like an object – be it a stone, cow or just a large clump of grass – each as indistinguishable as the next in the dark. In the mist, this place would be one of the toughest to navigate around. Taking a bearing would be almost impossible to get right, each direction looked so similar to the other; it was disorientating.

In Rannoch too, I'd learned about the local folklore that parents used to tell their children, of ghosts that are said to haunt the place as well as witches that morph into vampires when you kill them. Worst of all they say is the Cu Saeng, a monster so horrific that even a glimpse of it would kill you. The stories they told were, it is believed, to keep children from wandering out into the moorland unaccompanied. Stepping into a deep bog is no laughing matter – especially if you're on your own, and even more lethal if you're a small child. Despite my temporary jumpiness, looking around now I knew there was no wild cat sizing me up as a potential snack. The only thing to be wary of was the landscape itself. It's no coincidence that these so-called dangerous creatures, these legendary Cu Saengs and vampires, all have wild places as their dwellings. As humans we are scared by the wild and when the dangers aren't immediately obvious, we invent them as a way of keeping people away from anything that is deemed unsafe.

Happy to have reached this conclusion, though maybe a smidge sad to admit that the only exciting wildlife encounter I would be having here would be with the dormouse from earlier on, I began to back into my tent. I snuggled down into my sleeping bag, burying my head so deep that all I could make out was the rustle of the bag and the squeak of my mat. I surfaced only a couple of times to get a gulp of fresh air, but other than that I dozed in and out of sleep, with no more cats – big or otherwise – disturbing my thoughts.

In my eagerness to get moving the following day (I had to head back towards London for work) I had set the alarm for 7 a.m. and it woke me up with a start. At first I was reluctant to get up, it was so cosy in my down bag and I rested my eyes for a little while longer. It was still dark outside, being late autumn, the earlier signs of winter's approach beginning to manifest themselves.

As the tent walls started to reveal that daylight was almost breaking, I began to get undressed inside my sleeping bag, taking advantage of the warmth. When it was time to get out to put on my trousers, I prepared myself for the sudden drop in temperature and moved fast. I was eager to go outside and see what the day was like. Stuffing my sleeping bag away with the speed of a seasoned pro I unzipped the tent flap and peeked out. What a scene awaited me.

From my elevated position I really did have a fantastic view over some classic Dartmoor scenery. As a few orange light beams began to permeate the grey clouds, the straw in the fields below was instantly transformed into strands of gold; the high moorland that rose up in front of me looked like a palette of warm browns and yellows, suitably wild, yet stunningly beautiful. As the sun got stronger, the clouds began to dissipate and the remains of the vapours as they broke, lingered over the scene, floating lazily above it like veils of mist.

Beneath my feet a snake-like slow-worm (legless lizard – with no actual legs not consistently drunk!) slithered by. I felt overwhelmed by the beauty of it all and yet I was the only person in the whole world there to enjoy it, this was a special moment just for me and one I would treasure always. One thing was certain I realised, as I packed away the last of my gear, the early morning vista and the revelations I'd had about wild places had been eye-opening. I wanted more.

CHAPTER FOUR

NORFOLK COAST

Snow crunched under my boots with a muted squeak as I paced along the ground. Each footstep marked the pristine white with the dirty template of my sandy sole. In front of me, the usually well-trodden tracks were camouflaged, hidden by this unexpected coating of powder. I was breaking trail, the only walker in this ethereal scene. Below, the dunes thick with a pallid coat left by a recent flurry, offered shelter from the bitterness of the wind. I let my feet slide down into their depths, the walls of snow-covered sand rising either side of me, and immediately the air fell silent.

Methodically I pitched my tent, conscious that a salty mist was nudging closer to where I stood. All that remained of the sun was a fuzzy sphere, dimming to a sooty smear in the sky. The waves were rolling in and out with a reassuring regularity, but I could not pinpoint their location with any sense of certainty. I sat in the doorway of my shelter, unmoving, watching my breath merge with the vapours that clouded my vision. Just then, as if on cue, it began to snow.

It had never been my intention to wild camp in Norfolk. I was there off-season, doing some research for a walking guide on the ancient route of the Peddars Way, when the opportunity arose and I couldn't resist. The trail I had been following – an ancient thoroughfare which dates back to at least the first century AD – intersects with another long distance route called the Norfolk Coast Path and together they form nearly 100 kilometres of walking track. I'd spent several days exploring them when the weather took a real turn with wind beginning to spill in from the east – bringing with it the chill of the Baltics. Overnight the sand morphed from a warm gold to a hoary white as snow fell, then froze on top of it. Where the sea lay closest to the land, in inlets and creeks, it solidified into sheets of ice that shattered and cracked as the body of water shifted beneath its temporarily glacial surface. The sky transformed from a sapphire blue to an otherworldly grey, finger-like clouds grasping at the sun, its light casting mysterious shadows and shapes on the landscape.

I was due to head home that day – I'd got what I needed from the trip – but this inimitable mix of sand and snow was alluring. So instead, I found myself heading to the nearest outdoor store to buy some ice grippers for my boots. These are basically clip-on spikes that give added traction on frozen surfaces – something that in my entire life I never thought I would need right here in the flattest county in the whole of the UK. I packed my rucksack with some overnight things just on the off chance, and began walking once more.

Heading out from Burnham Deepdale, I made my way down to the shore. A collection of postcard-perfect wooden sailboats, lovingly hand-painted in pastel reds and greens, sat on the grassy banks. Despite it being only a little after midday, it already had all the indications that night was not far away. In the decreasing temperature and fading light, I turned to head west along the path.

Under the overhanging trees, the snow cover thinned. Above, the branches were caked in miniature heaps and every time a bird darted around it would dislodge one and sprinkle the powder onto the ground in a solitary flurry. Nautical instruments poked up out of the snow on the side of the path nearest the creek – life rings, anchors, rope and the orange of a round buoy, which looked brash and tasteless in this understated seasonal palette.

On the inland side, huge gardens stretched up to even bigger houses hiding the sea views from the streets behind. It seemed that here, water-adjacent residences were the reserve of the very rich alone. A little further and I reached something of a harbour. The raucous cries of a lone gull pierced the still air while the clank of metal on metal – a pulley hitting one of the boat masts – joined it in a tuneless discord.

Stacks of crab baskets lined the water's edge; tatty green twine seemed to keep them locked, making them resemble the skeleton frames of treasure chests dragged up from the bottom of the sea. I continued on a little further until the path became a raised wooden platform lifting me high above the muddy water of Brancaster Marsh. The wood creaked and groaned as I tiptoed along it, my ice grippers giving me much needed hold on its slick surface, scratching at the consolidated snow with each step. As I moved I could hear the partially frozen creek begin to splinter and split and watched as the liquid beneath squeezed its way through to form a puddle on the top.

I wasn't really sure I was heading out to try for a wild sleep at this point and certainly didn't think one I could realistically label 'extreme' could be on the cards. I had packed my full kit, but did not truly believe I would get chance to use it. Here in summer, the Norfolk Coast Path acts like a magnet to tourists. It's not that they intend to walk the whole length of it, it's just that it offers an easy and convenient access point to the sea that many come for miles around to visit. Now, without the sunshine or the warm weather, I found myself quite alone here. It didn't seem like the same place it had been just a day earlier.

I reached the end of the walkway and climbed over a stile onto a more solid path. I was now near the site of an old Roman Fort called Branodunum. Back when it was not only still standing but also occupied, it would have sat right next to the sea, and this would have also been an important harbour for the Romans, but since then, the water has receded. It seemed that the powerful waves – so unruly in the south around Lizard Point that it frequently steals land back from our reaches – had decided to abandon this pretty village, leaving it in the care of man... at least, for now.

Here the path led away from the water and after cutting through Brancaster began to climb ever so slightly up a rough country track. It might seem odd that a coastal path leaves the actual coast, but this happens more than once on this particular National Trail. It has a lot to do with rights of way (Marion Shoard would have a field day with that one) and that the marshland makes parts of the seaside route fairly treacherous. The fact that even somewhere as superficially tame and 'safe' as this, could actually hide a more dangerous streak, excited me.

As the slope levelled out I spied a cluster of three caravans tucked half into the hedges that lined my route. I stopped to see if I could see any signs of the occupiers but all I could make out was the flicker of a small flame. There was something quite mysterious and warming about seeing the firelight inside their tin walls upon which hoarthorn frost glistened in the sunset. I guessed that they were holidaymakers, come here in the off-season for a cheaper deal. It was funny to think that for them, in this weather, this was an extreme sleep.

I carried on through more fields, watching as the leaves glittered with hoar frost. My breath was becoming thicker as the temperature began to sneak down. I was glad of my warm jacket and – as I felt my foot slide on a hardened patch of ice – pleased I'd got the traction devices secured to my footwear.

I cut through a little patch of trees. Without leaves covering their branches they looked almost frozen in shock – as if they'd suddenly found themselves out there in the icy conditions without their coats.

BANG! The sound of a shotgun ricocheted in the air. Nearby farmers were out shooting pheasants. I winced as they fired again and saw a flock of birds rise up in the air. Perhaps it was this that shocked those trees into their unmoving state. Here, much to my disdain, I now had to join a tarmac road for a kilometre. I walked fast, hearing the rhythmic clink of my ice grippers as they hit the street beneath the layer of snow, and I willed the birds to stay put.

Soon I was in the hamlet of Thornham. A pub looked inviting and warm, but with some daylight still remaining and my plans still undecided I continued on to reach the sea path once more. This area is popular with birdwatchers, owing to its rich ornithologically-diverse residents, and they had clearly been out today in force. The path towards the reserve at Broad Water was a churned-up mix of mud, sand and snow. I kept to the outside of the track as I followed in their footsteps, feeling the chocolate-coloured water splashing up the back of my trouser leg as I walked on.

The sight of the lake made me stop in my tracks. Reflecting the silvery light above it, it looked like a giant piece of sheet metal. Catching the one bit of white light that was escaping the clouds, it was almost blinding.

I continued past the gate where a sign advised of an entrance fee. It seemed odd that you could be charged to watch a wild bird in its natural habitat – especially when you could see the same thing from this side of the man-made boundary for free. I moved on, not sure how I felt about this place and all its rules and restrictions. I already knew that here, much like the Lizard, wild camping is not legal. It's another place where you run the risk of getting moved along if caught, which, I thought as I plunged into a small patch of trees offering several possibilities for an overnighter, was a real shame.

Emerging from this little copse, I climbed past an old military bunker. It hadn't been used since World War Two – a time when the threat of our little island being conquered from the sea saw the government ramping up the number of defences at key points on the coast. Seeing the remains of this and further along the track, old spigot mortars, pill boxes and gun turrets, gives a fleeting glimpse into what wartime Britain looked like.

Soon I reached a warning sign. I was at the access area to Gore Point, a place reached only by exploring the land behind the sand dunes further out to sea, and negotiating a confusing network of small ponds and bogs. Sinking sand is not the only danger. Here, despite the impressive and friendly purples of sea lavender, it is a land not to be trusted. Shaped and continuously re-shaped by the tide, a few minutes into its reaches and you can find yourself stranded without warning. The hazard notice was a stark reminder as to how a wild space can exist even close to a seaside resort.

Further on and the dunes began to roll out to the now visible sea. Built by wind and water, these fluctuating mini hills curved round and framed the seascape. They were covered in a thick snowy coat, which so far was sticking even in the salty air – so brackish I could almost taste it, nature's own chip shop scent.

With each step, my foot crunched as the snow broke to reveal the sand. Grains stuck into the tread of my boots so that when I put my foot forward it sprinkled the white with a pepper of silt. I could not see the way ahead for more than a couple of metres now. The cold snap had brought with it a fog that was not in any rush to shift, so I was surprised when out of the miasma, the familiar shape of a beach hut materialised.

I had arrived at the outreaches of Old Hunstanton, neighbour to its more ostentatious sister, Hunstanton – a place where jellied eels, stripy deck chairs and candyfloss still rule. This older resort has a more stolid air. Here the beach huts are, for the most part, evenly spaced and well tended. Whereas in Hunstanton you might find a large Union Jack splashed on the door, here you are more likely to see natural wood and sympathetic restoration work.

I meandered past these quaint miniature homesteads. They go for tens of thousands of pounds in this part of the world and as I eyed up their little steps, their faux oil lanterns and big windows, I contemplated just how odd it must be to own a place in such a flawless location but never to be allowed to spend the night there. Here, even overnighting in a hut that you own is not allowed.

All at once I felt a pang of anticipation fizz through me. Whether it was the thickening mist, making every step feel like a journey into the unknown; the feeling of exclusivity at seeing this very rare combination of sand and snow; or simply the thought that by staying here I would be doing something forbidden – I can't say for sure – all I felt was that a sleep here would be wilder and more exciting than I'd anticipated.

I walked towards the sand dunes, climbing as they rose above the roof lines of the huts and moved a few steps further, picking out my route, feeling (perhaps undeservedly) like a pioneer. It was here that I slipped down into the dunes to erect my tent and it began to snow.

I nestled down to watch the way the light hit the flakes which tumbled from the sky as if a higher being was chucking buckets of confetti. The light was dimming and the temperature was beginning to drop – fast. I began to feel very cold, shivering uncontrollably as I searched in my bag for an extra layer. At the time, I didn't know the temperature (I later found out it had dropped to –11°C) but the wind seemed to be cutting through every scrap of fabric I placed on me as if it were nothing but a thin sheet of silk. My face felt frozen, stiff from the bitter breeze and my lips were dry.

I lingered a while, before trying to open a sachet of soup. It was like trying to do it with someone else's hands, my fingers wriggling about uncontrollably, refused to do anything I asked of them. I cupped my hands together and breathed on them slowly, trying to warm them into reanimation. They were still feeling numb but it gave enough of a boost of dexterity for me to be able to further rifle around in my bag and locate my thicker gloves and pull them on. With my hands in fists, I kept my fingers balled up to share the little heat they had.

Outside I could hear the cries of a fulmar hidden from view in the darkening surrounds. The scuffles of a rabbit hurrying through the sand caught my attention – it was likely trying to find some warmth too in this wintry weather. Beyond where I sat, I could hear the sea edging nearer to the dunes. Where I had pitched appeared to be well behind the tide line, but I mentally plotted an escape route should the worst happen.

Unlike at Lizard Point, where the waves crashed with such ferocity that they deafened me, it was the wind here that began to build up its strength, filling my ears with a powerful drone.

It was a struggle to do anything in the cold as it was, and I found myself moving much more slowly than I normally would, unpacking my sleeping bag and sorting out my kit at a speed just a tad faster than pause. The only other times I have experienced this level of frostiness were when out walking. The coldest I've ever been was in the Pennine Alps in Switzerland; I'd been snowshoeing among the jagged peaks that rose up like dinosaur teeth, biting into the sky with their serrated edges. There the temperature, with the effects of the wind chill, dropped to a ridiculous −35 degrees C. My eyebrows and eyelashes had frozen, even my hair had begun to solidify into icicle-like streaks. All my food was so hard with frost that I couldn't take a bite and the boiling water I had poured into my bottle less than an hour earlier had become a block of ice. Yet because of the very labour-intensive uphill activity, I had felt oddly warm. Now, on the fringes of a flat beach, open to the elements, battered by the winds that were gaining power with every gust, and not moving I felt chilled right to the bone. It was a perfect example of how extreme sleeping got its name. In most outdoor activities in the severe cold, you keep warm by moving around, but sleeping outside in cold weather is extreme because by lying still, you cannot warm yourself up and are more prone to succumb to the elements.

I didn't dare take off any layers – you're always supposed to strip to your thermals when getting into a down bag so that the feathers can trap the warm air close to your skin – and wrapping the fabric around me was not making much difference. So I decided to get out of my tent and move about a bit to get my blood pumping.

At first it was hard to force myself to stand up; the murk had completely closed in around me now and I did fear that straying from my tent too far would cause me to lose it. But once up, I began to pace backwards and forwards to warm up, followed by jumping on the spot, which turned into star jumps and spotty dogs, until finally I found myself doing a bizarre dance routine, whilst in between movements, I blew on my hands. I might have looked crazy had there been any passers-by about, but I did feel a little warmer.

Realising that was the best that I could hope for, I dived back into my tent and began stripping off layers ready to zip myself into my sleeping bag. As soon as I removed my walking boots I realised just how cold my feet had become.

I couldn't feel one half of my left foot from my big toe right down to my heel. I rubbed the foot between my hands hoping to warm it slowly. As it began to come alive, it burned with a stinging intensity and I flinched. I continued for a while longer then snuggled down into my bed trying to think warm thoughts.

I tried to picture that I was actually bedding down somewhere more tropical, perhaps a nice little sandy cove in the Caribbean, rather than on the eastern fringes of the UK. Then I reminded myself why I was there. The sights I'd seen today, where parts of the ocean had actually frozen, the waves cracking rather than breaking in the brisk weather and the sand dunes becoming snowy slopes, had given this place a whole new character and one that – despite the cold feet – I would have been very sorry to have missed.

Still shivering I reached inside my bag again and found my fleece and insulated jacket. I pulled both of them on and squeezed back into my sleeping bag. Closing my eyes tightly, I lay for several minutes, willing my body to get sleepy so that I would start to warm up naturally. It just wasn't happening. With the wind whistling through my tent I could feel it finding its way into my layers like a sneaky intruder. My hands were nearly as cold as before – I needed to place them under my armpits to get them to begin to defrost. Worst of all however, was my face. I had kept my woolly hat on, which helped to keep my ears protected from the breeze, but my neck and nose were stinging. Worse still, my teeth seemed to feel cold and even my eyes. I opened them and felt around for my bag for what would have to be the final time. I was running out of things to put on.

In the zip in the lid, I found my buff – a piece of seamless fabric tubing to wear round the neck. I pulled it over my head and my neck and felt it instantly remove the chill. Lying back in my bag, I pushed the fabric further up my face, until it covered my nose and most of my cheeks too. By the time I had pulled the toggle on the ruffle at the head of the bag around me, only my eyes were showing. I felt like a sleeping ninja. Yet still, in spite of all this help from proper kit, built for purpose, I felt cold.

I thought about how close I was to one of those beach huts, those twee little shacks that looked warm just in their demeanour alone, but they now felt like a million miles away. A place I never thought to be anything but predicable and safe was showing me its wild side – and it was not holding anything back.

I don't remember falling asleep. I felt like I was awake for most of the time, finding new positions to move into, each one exposing a new part of me to the colder side of the tent. Twice I mistakenly moved my arm out of the confines of my bag and dozed off – waking up with a numb appendage. As time slowly crept by, the wind began to die down and as if someone was fiddling with the sound levels, the balance of noise from the waves began to increase, eventually drowning out the gusts of wind and the flapping of the outer sheet of my tent. When the darkness was no longer complete, when I felt that dawn was nearing, I decided to have a peek outside.

The mist from the night before had cleared away, and the sky was a strange mix of dark and light, as though someone had tried to water down the black and what remained was an inky, blotting-paper type of smudge. Now the moon was visible, though fading slightly as the morning light nudged it to the background.

To my right the sand dune was coated with a deep thicket of marram grass which rustled in the light breeze. These hardy plants have a rhizomatic network of stems hidden deep underground – a complex web that helps them survive even when the dunes they live on move. I felt they were a little like the Norfolk coast itself: superficially docile, uncomplicated, and easy to dismiss as tame and 'soft' after just one quick look. But on closer inspection, you discover just how multi-faceted a place it really is, from unstable sands and extreme temperatures, to treacherous seas that drown the land and crumbling cliffs; all the layers, twists and turns it's made of remain for the most part, hidden from view in this eastern extremity of the country.

It was still ice-cold, perhaps more so after the clear night that had exposed this section of coast to unmitigated freezing conditions. I pulled myself back into the tent and tried to doze for a few more minutes, knowing at the back of my mind that I would need to get up and move on soon if I were to escape the place without being chastised for camping out.

A crunching sound startled me into actually making a move. I hurriedly packed away my kit and began removing my many layers. When I finally emerged and began pulling down my little structure, a seagull was sitting next to me on the dune, pecking away at the snow to try to reach the sand and presumably, any insects that lurked there under its feet.

Looking around I noticed that the snow still lay on the sand, stretching nearly all the way out to sea – despite the brine. As I climbed to the top of the dune I could see something large almost dancing in the air, its neon colours eye-catching. Kite surfers were out enjoying the crowd-free sands and I watched a pair of them in a graceful ballet while flocks of confused fulmars swarmed above, intrigued and a little terrified by the huge, flying canopies.

Making my way back on the path, I was pleased to be moving again and getting my blood flowing. I experienced a level of satisfaction that is difficult to explain. I had added another wild camp to my count that hadn't even meant to be, a spur of the moment sleep in a landscape that, strictly speaking, was out of bounds. I had also surmounted the hurdle of my first proper winter camp and was basking in the glory of surviving such a feat in (relative) comfort.

The path near the huts had remained hard and compacted, making the walk out more akin to a glacier hike than an easy seaside stroll. As I left the beach the snow began to thin until, reaching more of the built-up area, I noticed that most of it had melted away. Still cold but definitely happy, I felt like I too had experienced the sun shining on me and my quest.

CHAPTER FIVE

CADAIR IDRIS

It was nothing more than a whim that took me back to Wales. Two months after Norfolk, when most of the frost had thawed, I was funnelling down the M6 car-singing loudly as ever, when I spotted the M54/A5 turn-off. It seemed to glitter tantalisingly in the sunlight, calling out to me like a beacon that was hard to ignore.

Despite the tick, the sunburn and a – let's be honest – pretty hellish baptism of fire into the world of wild sleeps at the start of this venture, something drew me back there. Perhaps it was the hills desperate to prove to me that they could be more hospitable, maybe it was my growing addiction to these rough nights out, perhaps it was some kind of connection to the Big Country running through my veins that my parasitic tick left behind when I plucked it rudely from my side – I don't know.

At first I ignored it, turned the music up and belted out the next line, but then I found my voice trailing off as the familiar countdown strips appeared, demarking that if I was going to make this turn off, it was now or never.

I was still undecided as I hit the final warning that the turn-off was imminent. As the exit lane began stretching out to my left and before I even had time to work out just what or why I was doing this, I swerved at the last minute.

MEEEP! The car behind fired off his horn loudly – for several seconds longer than necessary – and I looked in my rear-view mirror to see the ruddy face of a middle-aged businessman cursing me despite being at more than a safe distance away. I simply waved and smiled.

Several minutes passed as I bombed down the much less frenetic tarmac lanes of the A road, when I suddenly realised that my reckless driving now had to result in the formulation of a plan. Where was I going? A serendipitous services sign flashed up on the side of the road and I pulled in to grab a coffee.

Newly caffeinated and feeling better now I had my road atlas in front of me, I followed the friendly line of the A5 with my finger, looking for something familiar.

Dolgellau. The name leapt out of the page immediately. Even though I'd grown up in the north of this country and am used to the seemingly limitless amount of saliva needed in order to pronounce place names correctly, I've always been impressed with the number of Ls the Welsh manage to cram into a single word. But my fascination doesn't end there. For me, the thing that sets me apart from 'foreigners' (though don't mention I was born on the wrong side of the border if anyone asks) is the way that Ls are pronounced differently depending where and how they fall in a word. Get two of them together and it's a 'TH'; just one and it's 'L' as in English; but put two together at the start of the word – as in Llandudno or Llangernew and suddenly the rules go out the window and you pronounce those two Ls with a hard, spit-inducing 'LCH' sound. That of course is the rule in the north. Cross slightly further to mid-Wales and the two Ls are uttered differently still – sounding more like an English person who refuses to take part in the linguistic version of pronunciation roulette. Don't even get me started on what happens if you're in the south, by the coast or in the valleys! It's because of these idiosyncrasies that I love the place. Knowing them allows you to breeze into a shop with the air of confidence at being an 'insider'.

The last time I'd been to Dolgellau was with a photographer called Bob. He'd insisted on pronouncing the name of the town we were heading to as 'Dolly geloo' much to my embarrassment. It made this sleepy Welsh town suddenly sound like an Australian suburb in Greater Sydney, full of sun-wrinkled outback men in leather vests, rather than rain-paled Welshmen in cagoules. How glad I was on my visit this time that I was alone with no one to show me up. I would present myself at the camping shop as an equal, as one of them and together we would laugh at the people like Bob who mispronounced the place names.

What I had forgotten of course was that – as is so often the case with these preconceived scenarios I like to create in my head – things rarely go according to plan. This is especially true when the shopkeeper has changed the rules and suddenly greets you with a 'Croeso. Bore da', and all my primary school Welsh flashes before my eyes with such speed that the only thing I can pick out clearly enough to say with some authority is 'How much is this banana?' and potentially – though perhaps not quite grammatically correctly – ask how many siblings he has. Attempting to formulate a suitable reply along the lines of 'Bore da, sut ydych chi... Llan... coed... llanfair pwll gwyn... gogo... goch' (a combination of hello, how are you and a jumbling of random place names), I wimped out and opted instead for a mumbled response in English. I straightaway noted the two 'real' locals behind me convert their conversation to the Celtic tongue I clearly lacked, to alert me to the fact that I was not, nor never would be, part of their exclusive club. After my dismal failure to connect with my adopted roots I brought a small gas can and fled in case I should mistakenly attempt to say goodbye but accidently compliment him on the size of his conkers or something equally inappropriate.

I had set my sights on a camp on Cadair Idris – allegedly the second most popular mountain after the country's highest peak. With a craggy summit, views over to some of the best scenery in southern Snowdonia and a huge glacial cirque which holds a massive lake, it certainly is a looker. But none of these draws were the reason I had singled it out for my next nap.

Though many hills and high places have spawned a plethora of legends, none are quite as ominous as those that abound on Cadair Idris. Folklore states that anyone who attempts to stay a night on its summit, will either go mad, become a poet or – perhaps the most important one that still manages to slip to the third rank in this list – die.

With most people thinking my extreme sleeping series was some bout of temporary madness, I could dismiss the first prediction. Of course, death was certainly something to give pause for thought. But, I reasoned, as I grabbed the last-minute 'go bag' that I keep in the boot of my car (a rucksack packed with clean walking gear and emergency kit for an overnight camp – should a last-minute opportunity ever arise... or a stupendously long traffic jam get a tad out of hand), a boost in the poetry department would always be a welcome string to my bow. With that, I slammed the car door shut and headed up the path through the trees.

Within minutes rain began to fall, hitting the hood on my jacket with a loud ping and I hoped this wasn't a sign of the evening taking a turn for the worse. Aside from the worrying trio of things that could go wrong on this summit, another slightly worrying Celtic legend tells us that this is the roaming place of Gwyn ap Nudd. Not a local farmer, you understand, but the Lord of the Underworld no less. He is said to patrol this peak with his pack of hounds whose howls can only be heard by those just about to be taken.

Suddenly, the yelp of a small Jack Russell startled me from under my Gore-Tex. Clearly not a hound of the underworld – though I've met a fair few Jack Russells who I'd hesitate to relieve of that title – this curious little mutt began hopping around my boots, wagging his stump of a tail excitedly.

'Bad up there,' said a voice. I looked up to see a man dressed in an odd combination of tweed and gaudy anorak shuffling down the hand-hewn stairs in the forest floor.

'Blowing a hoolie I'd say,' he added, water dripping off the brow of his hat onto the end of his reddened nose. 'I wouldn't go further if I were you. You going up still?'

As I struggled to formulate some kind of answer, he decided he didn't need one and continued the conversation as if I wasn't even there.

'Damn silly to continue,' he shook his head, sending a shower of second-hand raindrops shooting from the rim of his flat cap. 'You take my word for it,' he added as he and his dog vanished into the trees from where I'd come.

I trudged on despite his warning, being the stubborn sort that I am, his pessimism merely making me more determined to continue on my quest. The ground underfoot became increasingly waterlogged as I emerged from the trees and traced the path along the river. It was difficult to tell whether the sound of fast-flowing water came from the watercourse to my right or from the sky above.

In the three times I had been to Cadair before this day, every single one of them had had weather like this. Not just a drop of rain when the hope of sun was perhaps a faint possibility, but proper British rain, unashamedly globulous, and accompanied by thick, impenetrable grey clouds sucking out daylight like a kind of murky blotting paper.

The first time, I'd been a child, so simply refused to be heaved out of the car by my ever-patient father. The second time, when I was a little older, a friend and I decided we would walk up just to the lake. We were ill-prepared and foolishly carried handbags rather than rucksacks, clutched onto hoodies rather than waterproof jackets and for nourishment could boast a can of Pepsi and half a packet of Trebor Softmints. The weather chucked it down again and thankfully put an end to our disastrous attempted ascent about halfway through the forest. The third and final time before this was with the aforementioned Bob. We optimistically thought it was a passing flurry, over and done with in half an hour at most. So convinced were we that we even popped into the hotel at the foot of the mountain for some afternoon tea and scones, believing that somehow when we left, a Bahamas-like sunshine would be blazing outside. It wasn't, and we spent two days walking around with our heads down having nonsensical conversations as we each struggled to hear the other through our rustling hoods.

So it came as no surprise that day as I climbed higher, that the way ahead was thick with a claggy mist. I didn't mind that already I was wet through even to my underwear. I cared not that my hair had plastered itself to my face so that I resembled an extra in a BBC adaptation of a Jane Austen novel. No, what really got to me now was that all my friends – many of whom would only go near a mountain if it was under the bribe of a free pint and the promise that it would burn 3,000 calories in just under four hours of walking (a lie you are free to use yourself if you need it), had seen it bathed in the kind of blue sky and sunshine of the type reserved for places that end with the syllables 'biza', 'dorm' or 'bella'. These were people who didn't give two hoots whether or not they could see the summit or the crags reflected mirror-like into the lake below – just whether or not their beer was cold at the end. Yet I, a lover of all things hilly, had been denied ever clapping eyes on it other than in photos... and that day looked like it would be no exception.

Part of me had hoped that because this was an unplanned raid on this mountain, I might have caught it unawares and glimpsed it before it managed to hide under its cloudy shroud – but it was not to be. Now, as the way ahead levelled off to a flattened plateau, and the water came into view, all I could see was a wall of cloud hiding what should have been an incredible summit view.

It's from here where the peak gets its name. The mountain's steep slopes rise up around the back and side of the lake forming a grit amphitheatre of steep slopes and scree resembling – some will tell you – a giant chair. Or more correctly, a giant's chair. Cadair Idris – literally means the Chair of Idris – Idris being a giant who local legend has it would sit here and gaze at the stars in the night sky.

I knew that this was definitely a prime spot for a camp, but my sights were set a little higher. I began on the path that skirted round to the left with a sharp pull uphill of a couple of hundred metres. In the good weather, it's a little tiring; in the rain now, with a tent and stove adding to the weight in my rucksack, it was painful.

Spending the night here was always going to be a challenge, what with giants, hounds from the underworld and the threat of death by poetry... or whatever it was; but what with the lessening visibility in the early evening and the increasing regularity with which I was getting hail in the eye, this was becoming a battle – between me and mountain. And I was damned if I was going to let it win.

I struggled on up, the wind increasing and whistling through the edge of my hood, echoing loudly in my ears. I knew I had neared the top when the ache in my legs began to subside as I started to skirt the edge of the mountain. Knowing there was a huge drop down to my right I slowed my pace, grabbing where I could onto the spikes of rock that protruded every now and again from the slope, like fingers trying to grasp at my jacket.

I knew that it must be around 7 p.m. but even in early spring, it was much darker than it should have been. As I took a minute to reflect on this observation, toying with the idea of checking my watch to offer my eyes something of a change of scenery from the endless gloom, I felt my foot slip beneath me and frantically grasped around for one of those otherworldly spikes to steady myself.

As I jerked forwards, I got the feeling that this was definitely a 'close one'. Under the front sole of my right boot there was nothing but air and I realised, with a sudden and uncontrollable fluttering in my stomach, probably a hell of a lot of it. My left boot wasn't on much sturdier ground either, its rubber rand balancing precariously on a rock resting on the brink of the cliff face. The only thing that was solid was the thick spine of stone I'd manage to wrap a couple of fingers of my left hand around – just. The wind whipped up into even more of a frenzy as I fought to prevent myself from fully comprehending the predicament I was in.

Taking a deep breath, I gulped hard and wished for a split second that if Gwyn ap Nudd, the Lord of the Underworld was thinking of making an appearance anytime that evening, he should probably get a move on as I could really have done with a hand. Once it became apparent that help – from the spiritual or physical world – wasn't going to materialise I leaned my body backwards just a couple of centimetres. Happily the weight of my rucksack did the rest, tipping me towards the safety of more solid ground, and once I found more purchase under my fingers, I heaved myself backwards and began breathing normally again.

Shaken from my brief brush with danger I edged a few more steps forward only to be met with a sudden gust of wind. This was getting ridiculous. I knew I needed to stop or soon I wouldn't have to guess which of the three fates awaited me that night. I nervously crept on till I found a flatter section of ground, away from the edge and sheltered a little by some rocks.

I opened my rucksack and began rifling around in it for my tent, but nothing felt large enough to be it. With the rain pouring down, opening the top any larger than a slit would fill the rucksack faster than a newly-opened express register in a supermarket on a Saturday. So I performed what can only be described as a keyhole search in my bag for roughly five minutes.

There was the plastic lid and metal base on my stove, the sleeping mat, a worryingly-thin sleeping bag (well this was my emergency kit after all), a first-aid kit, some broken cereal bars – now feeling more like packets of dust, a melted and re-hardened contorted Snickers bar, a duvet jacket, some gloves and some odd sort of sausage-thin fabric wedge... oh no! As I moved my fingers over it another time, it quickly dawned on me that the wedge was actually the thing I was after. Only it wasn't a tent – it was a bivvy bag.

Now I love sleeping in a tent in the rain. The reassuring zip door, the sound of droplets tapping on the roof as you're cocooned safe and dry within, a place to stow and dry off some of your wet kit while the storm rages on outside. Love it. I have a friend though who hates it. Well actually, if I'm honest I have more than one.

Some people hate tents even when the sun shines and it's in their own back garden – 'there might be spiders', 'there's no toilet' or just 'why do it?' This particular one has a more specific reason: he happens to be over 6-feet 10-inches tall and equates sleeping in a normal tent to sleeping in a coffin. I've seen him lie there all night with his tent door open, needing to have fresh air and a look at the night sky to even be able to fall asleep. Then he complains when he has a stiff neck in the morning. I, understanding and ever-sympathetic comrade that I am, have no time for his excuses.

But when it comes to bivvy bags in the rain – I'm suddenly on the side of the haters and complainers.

A bivvy bag is effectively a waterproof sack just big enough to cover you in your sleeping bag and nothing else. There's no porch to cook in, no way you can hang kit up inside to drip dry, and as for manoeuvrable space to do a simple task like read a book – forget about it, that's just a pipe dream. In warm weather, most bivvy users will leave the head flap open so that you use it as a glorified sleeping bag cover, getting you as close to nature as possible while stopping you from getting wet with morning dew. You have the stars as your roof this way and if you're worried about bugs, normally there's a thin bug shield you can do up that still allows you to see out. In the height of summer, with the right light, sleeping in a bivvy can be close to perfect.

But in the rain, where you have no option but to zip yourself completely inside, claustrophobia can quickly kick in. I cursed myself for not checking my go-bag before I left the car, and again for not packing a tent when I made it up in the first place.

Resigned to this sorry state of affairs I began to secure it to the ground and opened out my sleeping bag inside it. My clothes were plastered to me and I would need to take them off lest I transform my down-filled bed into a sopping pouch of wet feathers. I looked at my bedraggled excuse for a camp, shoved my deformed Snickers into my mouth and sighed.

I had a Plan B... with B in this case, being for 'Bothy' – a very basic mountain hut maintained by volunteers for walkers to use. However, I was a little loath to use it. After my recent sleeps on the flatter landscapes of Dartmoor and Norfolk, this particular trip was supposed to be about getting closer to higher and more dramatic mountainscapes, sleeping that bit closer to the wild, and not just a night in a stone shelter. Just then a gust ripped up the fabric from the ground and I raced over to secure it, dropping my much-needed chocolate into a muddy puddle. It was then I decided that B actually stood for Bloody Brilliant.

Making the decision to decamp to a place where I could actually move around in relative dryness perked me up no end. I packed away all my gear into my waterlogged backpack with a renewed purpose – I didn't even break my smile when a bivvy peg refused to budge and sliced through the side of my finger – all this discomfort would soon be forgotten and relegated to the realms of another story to tell another night.

As I left, I noticed that the mist had become even more sinister. I honestly thought a wolf (or more appropriately an underworld hound) howling at the moon wouldn't seem out of place. I checked the map and began to walk forwards to where I was convinced the bothy was. So engrossed was I in my new destination and all the hot drinks and happiness it would bring, that it took me a few minutes to realise that I was going downhill not up.

How had that happened? I was sure I was heading the right way. Tired and hungry, I turned a full 180° and went back uphill, only to find myself going back down a few seconds later. Disorientated and desperate for a cup of tea I tried again and found myself finally ascending once more.

The darkness was closing in and a frosty breeze tickled at my nose. I was sure that I was going to see the unmistakable outline of the bothy looming ahead any minute, but every time I saw something promising and the rocks would spread out as I approached, it would come to nothing.

Then the worst happened – I began to descend again. Somehow I had passed the summit and the emergency summit shelter without even realising it. Fed up and convinced that it would clearly be madness that would lead to my ultimate demise out here on Cadair Idris, I began to walk uphill once more. As I went, I amused myself by wondering out loud – always the first sign of madness – if perhaps I might be able to put this episode in a poem – perhaps a haiku. Then, as if out of nowhere, the trig point suddenly materialised in full view – so clear in fact, that I wondered how I could have ever missed it at all without stepping for a brief few minutes into an alternative reality. Either way, I was there. I had reached the top. I had no idea what it looked like buffered either side in grey cloud, but I was there. This meant, I realised with an inner joy, that the bothy was nearby too.

Through strained eyes I surveyed my surrounds. Behind me was ruled out because I would surely have noticed it. To my left was the gaping drop down to the lake below so an unlikely spot for a building, and in front – surely – was the way I had originally come up. It had to be to my right.

I now realised that the rain had steadied to a light spittle rather than the full-on downpour from before and I took a minute to remove my hood, stand on my pedestal and listen for signs of life. There were no howls of the death-signalling hounds, no rhyming couplets being chanted from another walker who had done an extreme sleep here before me and then been converted to a Cadair bard, and no giant snoring as he slept in his favourite chair below. I was definitely alone.

I cautiously paced a few steps to my right where I spotted a cluster of rocks. It wasn't the shelter but something felt right. I moved forward a bit – nothing. I retraced my steps then went a bit further on – still nothing. Then finally, I spotted it. I had practically been circling the damn thing for twenty minutes! It was nearly night and I had to look really closely to see it. Its construction from the local rocks meant it blended seamlessly into the surrounds, well hidden from the summit, but obvious and welcoming from where I now stood.

Inside, it was much bigger than I had anticipated. Two large central stone tables seemed to grow mushroom-like out of the ground. Straightaway I plonked my heavy rucksack on the nearest one. Bench-like platforms circled the edge of the large stone room, with a little light coming in from two cobweb-crusted windows, where a clearly thoughtful soul had seen fit to leave a full bottle of questionable yellow liquid on the windowsill. Another equally philanthropic person had left a half a bag of peanuts and an open pack of oatcakes next to it – a sure way to attract rats and mice. The benches were not very wide to provide good sleeping platforms (this was an emergency shelter rather than a normal bothy), but hearing the rain begin to pick up again, popping and pinging off the tin roof above, they looked to me as good as a four-poster bed.

Peeling off my waterproofs, I began to transform the stone shelter into my own personal drying room, the grey walls instantly covered by the bright reds, oranges and greens of my Gore-Tex. As I moved around the place in my base layers, steam coming from them as the warmth of the fabric met with the cold bothy air, I began to feel a chill. I snuggled into my duvet jacket which succeeded in making my nose envious as it dripped uncontrollably.

If there was ever a time for a cup of tea it was now and I soon fired up my stove feeling warmed – at least mentally – by the tiny orange flame. It's easy to take the little things for granted when you're back inside all the mod cons of your brick-built house, and be underwhelmed by simple pleasures. When you're sleeping out in a cold unheated shack, it's the little things that can really lift your spirits. So it was with unrivalled joy that I discovered that I had, in a stroke of genius that I'd clearly forgotten about, packed a small tea light candle and a couple of matches into the watertight bag that encased my first-aid kit.

The pleasure I got from watching its little orange flame flicker at the window was immense, comparable only to supping a hot peppermint tea. The night may not have turned out quite how I had planned, being surrounded by four walls rather than sleeping with my head poking out of a bivvy with the stars for a roof, but this seemed as near to perfect as a night out could get.

The menthol aroma filled my nostrils and the steam engulfed my eyes. I breathed heavily and felt a wave of sleepiness finally wash over me. I should have, just in case some other poor soul emerged in a similar situation as me, considerately moved my things into a more manageable cluster, rather than spread them haphazardly around the walls. But I felt more tired than ever and couldn't will my body to do anything more than slip into my sleeping back and scrunch up the ruffle around my head, so that I mummified myself in a feathery womb.

As I lay there listening to the increasingly louder taps on the roof and creaks that always come with older buildings, I felt heartedly reassured. The constant noise, though loud, was comforting. Despite my resolution to try to stay awake at least till midnight to see if a wave of creativity would spur me to pen a sonnet that would rival those of Shakespeare, I drifted off to sleep.

I woke to a change in the sound outside – or rather a lack of it. The constant dripping of rain had ceased, and other noises were now audible. I was sure I could hear a kind of scraping sound. The flame from my candle had died. 'This is it,' I thought, 'Gwyn has come to end it all for me.' All the scary and ridiculous horror stories I had ever heard from my childhood came flooding back.

Gone were the reassurances I'd got from deconstructing myths of big cats back in Dartmoor. Now, here, the only explanation for these scraping noises in my movie-addled brain was an axe-wielding maniac sharpening his blade on the roof of the bothy. I realised, with a certain degree of impressiveness, that my mind was clearly concocting a re-imagining of the classic urban myth where I go outside to investigate and a policeman is waiting to tell me not to look back, but to run. Yet I don't listen, look back and there, standing on the roof is a machete-armed killer holding in his hulking, bloody, outstretched arm the head of the walker I'd seen earlier, his little Jack Russell yelping underneath him.

Suddenly I woke up – really woke up this time – to the real sound of scraping outside. The only thing I could do to enable me to sleep again was go out and investigate – to confront my fears head-on for what I hoped would be the last time. I reluctantly unzipped my sleeping bag and stumbled around the bothy grabbing at items of clothing in a haphazard fashion and throwing them on. The result of this was that I was dressed like some kind of mismatched European hiker, with my fleece inside out, the leopard-print buff I wear for bed to keep my neck warm pushed up over my hair like an unfashionable bandana (think Bet

Lynch meets American eighties mulleted-rockers Poison), with bright-blue long johns tucked into down booties and plunged into brown hiking boots with the laces undone. It was nearly enough to make me rethink my plan, but seeing as I felt virtually wide awake, I reasoned I may as well take a look outside even if I was to meet my sticky end dressed like a poor man's Lady Gaga.

I couldn't find my headtorch. Instead, what I did find was the glow stick I keep in the outer pocket of my bag for emergencies (and the odd impromptu rave obviously, should I ever find myself in the wilds in the early 1990s). I felt simultaneously satisfied by the click it made to get its dayglow liquid filling activated, and mildly disappointed with the dim yellow strip of light it produced. Its muted tone gave the room an eerie glow, casting shadows onto the walls of objects I hadn't noticed in the daylight. It served to do nothing except – and this is the really annoying part – give out enough light to see my headtorch hanging off the edge of the stone table.

By this time, the scraping noise that woke me had stopped, but I crept towards the door regardless and grabbed my headtorch as I went. I listened for moment and was about to turn the handle when I suddenly had a bright idea. I wouldn't be the stupid person at the start of a film who walks out into the unknown unarmed. No, I would be prepared for my would-be attacker whether it be man, beast or poet. I stopped, reached beside the door, and grabbed one of my walking poles. Feeling more prepared for my fate and thinking that at least if I did meet my end, the papers would praise me for not facing the onslaught unarmed, I grabbed the door handle. I could see the headlines now: 'Crazy writer dies – but at least she went out fighting. Subhead: was one hell of a dresser.'

I slowly opened the door, flinching as it began to creak loudly – this would make any animal or killer in a 3-metre radius aware of my exact location. I decided to give it one big hard push – as calm and calculated as a member of the SAS – ensuring any would-be attacker standing behind the door would be knocked to the ground with the thrust of the action. But I misjudged and hit it with such a force that it immediately bounced back and whacked me on the leg. To add insult to injury, I didn't realise that in my haste to grab my stick, I hadn't fully pushed the clasps on the pole to keep it in place and the bottom half shot out behind me, clattering as it fell to the darkened bothy floor. It wasn't quite the desired effect, but to my relief, it soon became apparent that there wasn't a single soul around for miles. In fact, if death was still on the cards, it was only to be by my own embarrassment.

Though I now knew that whatever scraping sound I'd heard was more likely to have been a sheep scratching itself against the door, I realised I would have to turn around and check out the roof. Taking a deep breath I looked back and stopped dead in my tracks.

There was no killer there, no beheaded walker or accompanying dog; instead there was the most beautiful night sky I had ever seen. The firmament was so deeply black, it was like the velvety curtain a photographer would use in a studio; the stars, tiny holes pinpricked into the material and backlit to produce intense clusters of radiant white light. The rain had stopped and the moon was a bold crescent-shape so perfect it looked Photoshopped into the scene. I couldn't resist it, I tiptoed up to the trig point several feet away and looked down to see if Idris the Giant was indeed in his chair – surely if there was ever a night to put in an appearance this was it.

I looked down, but I was still alone. Alone except for the best view into the glaciated scoop of the cwm below where the whole night sky reflected in the lake beneath, placing me somewhere in the middle of two endless glowing vistas. As I trod softly back to the bothy, I caught a glimpse of a spider's web in the damp night air, the droplets of water from the former rain shower illuminated like crystal studs.

The fear and disorientation I'd felt minutes before had now gone the same way as the clouds and I smiled, feeling more reassured out in the open. The building that had provided me with the feeling of safety looked dark, but here outside, the landscape was welcoming and heavily lit by the moonlight. It was such a beautiful night I decided to take my stove outside to have a hot chocolate and watch the stars, paying homage to my no-show giant.

It wouldn't be long before the black melted away to a more hoary tone of grey so I went inside to grab my sleeping bag and bivvy, taking this long-sought opportunity to lie, as I'd wanted to, right on the summit with my head surrounded by nothing but stars.

I must have dozed off again, courtesy of my newly-contented state. I only know this because, what seemed like seconds later, something wet landed on my forehead. I tried to ignore it, blissful in a dozy condition. Then another landed on my cheek, followed by one on my lips and finally my nose. I opened my eyes to see thick, fat raindrops beginning to fall again.

'*Grrrr!*'

I heard a growl. The hounds were finally here... but these definitely didn't belong to Gwyn. Two boisterous yellow Labradors bounded up and began licking my face, making me instantly more soaked than the rain had. Behind them, a couple, securely clad in waterproofs, ambled towards me.

'Morning,' the man said, looking slightly perplexed. I felt my head and to my dismay realised that I hadn't taken off the leopard print buff from my hair.

'Y'alright,' I smiled, getting up with as much poise as I could muster. If they were going to judge me they may as well be treated to the full monstrosity that was my outfit.

'Been out here all night?' said the woman in a tone just bordering on mild horror as she eyed my down booties (or should I say booty since one had now gone AWOL in my sleeping bag).

'Oh yes,' I replied, then just to amuse myself added, 'I was looking for giants, don't you know.'

They shared glances as if deciding whether or not to laugh or call for the men in white coats.

'Well, can't stand around chatting all day,' I said and took my leave to the bothy with a theatrical bow.

I mused, as I reconfigured my fashion disaster into something slightly more presentable, that the legend had been true all along. Cadair Idris really had made me mad.

I retraced my footsteps down towards the lake and back onto the path that would eventually lead me through the forest and back to my car. Not once on that walk did I catch a glimpse of the summit as cloud had once more hidden it from me. But it didn't matter. I had seen it the way it was meant to be seen – at night, out in the open, from the best seat in the house.

And as I passed the time desperately trying to think of a word that rhymed with Idris to test out my heightened poetry skills, and failing miserably, I reassured myself that one out of three predictions coming true wasn't bad.

CHAPTER SIX

BLEAKLOW

It was hard to breathe. The thick, soupy mist that had been steadily building, now seemed to engulf me like smoke. It felt wet on my fingertips, so dense I could actually touch it. Behind me, the solid shapes of the two boulders known as the Wain Stones – my navigational aids – disappeared, concealed temporarily like some kind of elaborate magic trick. In front of me, as the wind stretched and pierced the fog, I could see something else, something shiny, and I knew I had to discover what it was. This was how I came across *Overexposed*, the wreckage of a World War Two American Superfortress Bomber.

Wedged between the two northern cities of Manchester and Sheffield, the Peak District National Park has long held a draw for outdoor lovers. There's a statistic floating out there on the internet that states it is the most visited park outside of Fuji National Park in Japan – though the authorities here say they have no idea where this factoid has come from. But even with that aside, the Peaks (as they're locally known) have a history with walkers. It was here, back in 1932 on the mountain plateau a few miles south of where I stood, that Kinder Scout, the highest hill in the area was the backdrop for a protest against wealthy landowners who had stopped people walking across this piece of countryside. Even before Marion Shoard heroically protested for the right to roam, these city workers were mounting a march. Sick of seeing this impressive high-moorland plateau from the built-up places they called home and being unable to legally access it, around five hundred walkers took part in a Mass Trespass. Those from Manchester were led by campaigner Benny Rothman and started at the Bowden Quarry in Hayfield; the others from Sheffield began in Edale. They met a little behind the summit on the small promontory of Ashop Head and celebrated their success. However, on their return five were arrested and sentenced to up to six months in prison – something that eighty years later has since been pardoned.

It's easy to see why they chose Kinder as the site for their protest. Much like neighbouring Bleaklow, it's the highest thing for miles. The mountains loom above the villages, quivering masses of gritstone seemingly held together by black peat. Water forms a network of vein-like rivers on the tops, then runs down into the villages, creating visual clefts in their otherwise impenetrable profiles that beckon you to conquer.

The Mass Trespass kick-started a serious rethink about people's right to roam. It led to the creation of National

Parks in the UK – the Peak District being the first in 1951 – and now great tracts of land previously out of bounds to the public are designated as Access Land, meaning wandering around both on and off the path is very much allowed.

The only beef I personally have with the authorities now is that they are still opposed to wild camping. The land on Bleaklow and elsewhere in the park is so expansive, so far-reaching and so empty that there's no real reason that responsible overnighting in tents should be illegal. Even though it's supposed to be the most visited of all the National Parks, being so close to where a huge bulk of the population lives, I've still managed to find vast swathes of it devoid of people – even in high summer. The main worry seems to be that its proximity to the cities might attract those who will do something irresponsible like start a fire, the consequences of which on this highly-flammable peat could be devastating – especially to the nesting birds who call this place home. I do hope that one day they might realise that, as on Dartmoor, allowing people to camp in the right way and actively encouraging it with some clearly-defined guidelines will help them protect the land better than any other high-profile campaign they could think of.

Rules are rules for now though, so I knew that for this particular camp I would have to be discreet. It was never my intention to find the aircraft wreck, I had simply decided to go there on my way back from visiting friends in Manchester – it was a way to sneak in a quick extreme sleep without much extra driving. My plan was to spend the night by the Wain Stones. These weather-scoured lumps of rock are marked on all the maps and look like two faces which from a particular angle, appear to be kissing. Spending the night near them would shelter me from the gusts of wind that often tear across this very high, but flat moorland. The stones would also be easy to find in a place that can so often change from tame easy walking (compared to mountains like Cadair) into a navigational nightmare. I also felt the loving sentiment would be a nice touch too.

I'd decided to approach them from the lesser-visited north end – away from the more commonly used lay-by on the Snake Pass Road from Glossop. Although it meant more of an ascent it would easily take me to the Wain Stones. Not managing to shake off my run of inclement weather, true to form it began to rain when I started up the hill. Even in dry conditions, Bleaklow's tussocks, hillocks and hummocks can be treacherous, requiring you to shout out expletives that end with a similar sound. The danger of bogs is very real and in wet weather the risk of sinking waist-deep in cold black mud increases dramatically. As I started my walk in the rain, the path sucked at my boots like a child trying to slurp all the flavour out of an ice-lolly.

The first bit involved cutting steeply uphill above a farm, easy but slightly tedious – particularly with a slick coating of previous rain. I continued to walk along the path, one moment balancing on what looked like solid ground, the next, sinking slowly and flailing about trying to pull myself out of it. Where I could, I skirted around the edges of the actual path, trying to avoid the mud. This was a good plan with two main drawbacks. The first was that so many people before me had obviously employed the same tactic, resulting in a mud-churned path so wide that going round the edge would have meant a walk twice as long as the one I intended. The second was that the whole of Bleaklow is essentially one giant muddy puddle in that type of weather anyway, as slippery as the main path if not more so. As the bogs got wider and the deep puddles bigger, there was nothing for it but to plough through.

Gaining height seemed to offer a way out of my predicament so I took a little run up the peat hag to my right (ground where peat is cut, not an ugly old woman!), managing to climb temporarily out of my peaty passageway. Despite the growing mist I could just about make out the land rising on the other side of the valley that I'd successfully climbed from. Black Hill dominates the skyline and from here, it appeared as an ethereal shadow of a peak before the growing vapour locked it away from view.

I continued to walk along the path, checking the map to make sure tiny features on the ground were in fact matching up with what I should have been seeing. Even though I knew that I would be passing the Wain Stones on my way to the trig point that demarks Bleaklow's true summit, I decided that with the weather as it was, it would be the safest approach. That way I could plot a bearing and there would be no way I would miss them – I didn't want another annoying episode of trying to find my planned bedroom as I had endured on Cadair Idris.

Just I was thinking how wild the weather was making this city-side wilderness feel compared to previous visits I'd enjoyed under sapphire-blue skies, I looked up to see a thick candyfloss wad of cloud descending rapidly on the views ahead. Then, the rain began to really fall. Slowly it removed footprints and any signs of footfall from previous walkers. It washed away traces of where I'd come from – turning any boot impressions into puddles, camouflaging any signs of a trail. Jumping onto a lower section of peat hag, I saw nothing but an intensifying fog.

Had it not been for the fortuitous placing of a Werther's Original in my pocket at the start of my walk, now found by mistake when searching for my compass, I might have begun to panic. This was not my first time in these conditions and I was much better prepared. As soon as I put the sugary sweet in my mouth – more as an afterthought just to get the thing out the way – I felt instantly better. It was as though the sudden shot of sticky carbs silenced any sign of the rising lunatic inside my head and forced me to take stock more calmly of what was going on.

Throwing on my warm jacket and plunging my damp hands into a pair of thick, waterproof gloves, I felt just a tad smug at how far I'd come in my ability to keep calm in this kind of a situation. Looking at the map, I realised that if I followed the path I was on, I would reach the summit eventually – providing I didn't deviate. Even at the worst-case scenario, I would reach it in the following fifteen minutes and if I didn't, I could always set up camp wherever I was.

I started to walk on again, developing windburn to my cheeks. As I moved forwards, the mist became patchier and the rain began to ease a little. Then the stack of stone on which the white trig sits appeared ahead. From here I could take a bearing and did so immediately, eager to be inside my tent and start drying off.

With my compass in hand, I picked my way towards the Wain Stones. I was walking very slowly and deliberately, purposely stamping my feet down in muddy patches of the path to make sure footprints were left should I decide to backtrack. It wasn't long before the smooching stones came back into view. I saw them for a second before they slowly disappeared again – but it was enough of a glimpse to spur me on and walking faster, I was soon upon them again. In the murk, from that angle they looked less like a happy kissing couple; I saw them now in my sodden state as more of a smirking sardonic twosome. I took a minute to shelter from the wind behind their faces and work out what to do next.

The rain had all but stopped and despite my early eagerness to erect my tent, I now felt compelled to take in a little more of the misty landscape. I looked at the two rocks and spotted a clear foothold on one of them in an otherwise smooth surface. Hoiking my way up it, I gripped tightly onto the stone as I was blasted by the wind and looked around. There wasn't much to see. I couldn't even make out the trig point I'd passed. As I began to climb down I looked up one last time towards the south side of the moor. For a split second, a shaft of sunlight appeared again and I saw something reflecting back at me from across the way. It almost looked as if someone was signalling me.

I clambered back down to the ground and grabbed the map. There was nothing in that direction except for Higher Shelf Stones summit and there was nothing shining about that. Then I remembered, *Overexposed*.

Our hills are littered with the wrecks of many an aircraft lost in the thick soupy fogs that often cling to the UK's high points. They disorientate pilots, causing them to lose control just for a second and nip the top of a summit, which results in them meeting an untimely end. There are hundreds of websites and even the odd book dedicated to listing these wrecks in meticulous detail. Sometimes all that is left is a small smattering of metallic pieces, barely recognisable as anything that used to fly. Occasionally there's more – perhaps a whole wing, or even something resembling an engine – so you're left in no doubt as to what it is you're looking at. However, out of all the wrecks out there, the best preserved is that of the *Overexposed*, an American RB-29 Superfortress Bomber that rests on Bleaklow's moors.

The story is a particularly sad one. The thirteen men on board weren't in battle, gunned down by enemy fire or shot down like war heroes. In fact these men made their fateful flight just after the war had finished. They were carrying payroll money and mail from one air base in Lincolnshire to another in Warrington, with no risk of gunfire or the sound of a German fighter plane beating down on them. The mission was a safe one and three days after making the drop, they were to head back home to the USA. Bleaklow, however, had other ideas. A thick mist descended on the peaks high above the town of Glossop. Their base was only twenty-five minutes away, but they never arrived. They flew too low, and before they knew it, hit the top of this vast expansive moorland and their whole world was shattered. The bodies were removed and returned to loved ones, but the wreckage remains as the terrain is too dangerous to remove everything safely. Back in its glory days, the aircraft was used for photo reconnaissance work, hence its moniker – *Overexposed*. I felt myself shiver.

I'd read about this before and it seemed tantalisingly close now – I had an urge to see it. Despite the limited visibility I knew where I needed to head to, and so, tasting wet mist in my mouth, I began to leave the safe site of the Wain Stones and make my way out towards this glistening metallic object. Now I was well away from any semblance of a path, the ground began to disintegrate around me. I knuckled down at the slippery slopes, edging nearer to the wreck while the fog thickened around me. A particularly high peat hag now blocked the way forward.

I took a running jump, raising my arms towards the top as I did. For just one glorious second I felt the grass under my fingertips then it was over, the cold wet patch of mud was right under my belly as I lay tightly against the slope grasping around with my hands for solid ground to cling to. I could feel the water saturating my top and began frantically moving my legs to try to propel my body upwards. Mud pellets were flying all over the place as I struggled on relentlessly – adamant in my refusal to admit defeat – until finally, summoning all the upper body strength I had, yanked myself up to the top.

The rain had stopped but I still felt drops against my right-hand side. I looked down and realised that I had somehow manage to twist the tap on my hydration bladder (that was holding my water in an accessible bag in my backpack), so that the tube for easy drinking was now dripping away all the water I needed, onto my mud-encrusted chest.

Resembling a Glastonbury attendee circa 1998, I continued on a little longer until I could just about make out a sliver of aluminium in the murk. It looked like part of a wing, or maybe the side of the craft. A few steps on and I found more scattered parts of the wreck – the sliced-up pieces of a tail on one side, the huge chunk of a rusted engine the other, the porthole shapes where the glass used to be, a virtually intact wing. Among all this was a simple memorial stone dedicated to the crew who lost their lives that fateful day over sixty years ago.

I walked towards what would have been a window and touched it lightly with my fingers. It was icy cold and I instinctively pulled my hand away and shook it to warm it up. The fog lingered there, framing the scene like an atmospheric sepia snapshot.

The place had a real sense of presence. It felt wild, but this intrusion of the man-made gave it a feeling unlike any other place I'd been before. I wasn't ready to leave it, I wanted to see the pieces of the past merge into the night, so I began to pitch my tent. I trod softly around the pieces of the plane and as I did the mist began to thin. Suddenly, among the monochrome fragments, I spied paper poppies. Not just one, but a sea of red coated some of the engine and poked through the portholes. It was a glimpse of Technicolor in the dusk. These symbols of hope, or love for those lost, felt comforting and I decided to select a spot to sleep just behind the memorial stone, keeping a respectful distance from the debris.

As soon as my tent was up and my wet layers peeled away – not to mention a hot drink warming my hands – I felt somehow at peace. Everything around me was silent. I could hear the whisper of the wind as it shot through the pieces of metal, rediscovering flues and chutes that were left behind. Right at the start of this mission, if I had come here first, this place would have probably spooked me. I would have thought of ghosts wandering the moorlands as they became lost in a mist that, for them, would never lift. But here, now, thinking of the hardworking crews that would have mustered together to try to help the fallen, I felt a true sense of caring and even tenderness, even up on this scarred and brutal land. It was as if the wild was allowing me to see something of its softer side, even at a site that was associated with something so violent. I was glad that Bleaklow had offered up this extra experience. Originally this was just to have been an outdoor sleep conveniently near to a main road, coffee shop and supermarket. I never expected to find this, a place with a real heart – wild though it was. That thought helped me feel at ease as I climbed into my sleeping bag, so much so that I quite quickly fell asleep – much quicker than I thought I would – even to the point where I left the tent flap open.

Movement outside stirred me back to life and I rubbed my eyes to see what was going on. Any previous fears were replaced with a curiosity to see what critter could be making this noise. I felt oddly unconcerned even if it happened to be a ranger, clued up on my game and coming to expel me from his land. I lay there, watching my breath vaporize in front of me as a cloud of frosty air. The mist outside still lingered, the stars hidden; only the moon was winning the battle to pierce the clouds with its dim glow. The remains of *Overexposed* were obscured save for one piece directly in front of me where I could make out the unnaturally smooth curves of its structure. In front of it, a rabbit bobbed into view twitching its nose. Unconcerned by my presence, it hopped around indifferently before blending back into the darkness with a flash of its white tail. I breathed normally once more, pleased about the visit, then snuggled further into my sleeping bag and waited for sleep to find me again.

An eerie glow that I could only assume was a muted sunrise stirred me awake the next morning. I dressed quickly in my little tent, doing the kind of wiggle necessary to put clothes on in such a confined space. I knew that I was nearer to the Glossop side of the hill and people often check out key spots in the morning, so I wanted to disassemble all signs of my camp quickly. I crawled out of the tent to see if the morning's half-light would reveal any more of Bleaklow's secrets. The mist still hung low, impasto blobs of it colouring the pale sky, but it was thinning.

I scanned the scene around me. It was still early, no sign of other walkers, no campers who had flouted the rules like I had; just a comforting stillness in this odd scene of man-made and natural landscape – so violently combined, yet somehow looking like they had grown comfortable with each other's presence.

From here I could once more make out the Wain Stones. The mist was definitely lifting now, as if it had only come to conceal my night-time camp. Before I left, I wandered over to the summit of Higher Shelf Stones, the nearest high point to the wreck and right on the edge of the high plateau. The wind whistled in my ears as I walked over to it and took a seat on the trig point where I sat for several minutes looking over the place where I had slept the night. I marvelled once more at how much land there was up there, before looking down to the houses in the valley below. There was more than enough to go round I reckoned, even if every person in Manchester and Sheffield headed up here on a weekend together.

Peering back at the wreckage, now much more clearly visible, I was amazed at how well tended it was, how people must regularly come and visit to replace the paper poppies when they had faded or torn in the harsh conditions. It was obvious that people still really loved this wild place and respected it just as much as they did eighty years ago when the Mass Trespass took place.

I looked down at my feet to see a poppy had come loose and blown off. Bending down, I picked it up and headed over to the wreckage to replace it. As I hooked the green stem through the metal, completing the wreath of flowers at the end of the wing where it had been ripped away from the body of the craft, I felt that these man-made poppies in the wilderness were quite symbolic. To me they showed that tender thoughts and actions could be born out of an urban environment; that although the wilderness could be brutal, it could also have a profound effect on those it touched.

With that, I turned to walk through the muddy puddles, and when the mud splashed up at me and the rain began to pour once more, I didn't mind a bit. Now, like the Wain Stone faces I was passing, I simply smiled.

CHAPTER SEVEN

PENDLE HILL

The temperature was beginning to drop. The evening was clear. All around me the sky was becoming a layered pattern of purple, pink and white clouds with a ribbon of muted grey fading to silver behind. The witching hour was approaching, sundown bathed the fellsides and rooftops in an aptly Halloween-orange glow. Tonight I wasn't even going to bother with a tent, so I lingered longer on the summit of Pendle Hill, watching and waiting for something to happen.

Two things were occurring at this point that confirmed I must be crazy – clearly a residual effect from Cadair Idris. The first was that I was up north despite it being nearly the last day of October in the full throes of autumn – a time when the weather can range from anything from rain to typhoon, snow to blizzard or breezy to galeforce. The second was that I had come for this unplanned outdoor escapade to Pendle the day before it becomes virtually covered with visitors.

Pendle Hill is synonymous with one thing – witches. And not just any old witches, not the theatrical ones with big warts and green fingers, the type which children like to dress up as when 31 October rolls around. These were real wise woman and their families who all lived in the area and four hundred years ago became embroiled in the biggest witch trials that England has ever seen, resulting in the death of twelve people. Legend has it that their spirits haunt the massive peak that looms large over their former villages and come Halloween night, many people journey here from all over the UK and even further afield (some in fancy dress) to host séances and scare each other silly with ghost stories in a mass night-walk activity.

I wasn't sure if I believed in the ghosts and it was purely a case of serendipitous timing that I happened to be passing by Pendle. I had some spare time on my hands before I needed to head back to London. This was one extreme sleep I couldn't resist.

I love this time of year; the colours, the way the landscapes we thought we knew so well become hues of gold and amber, the sounds of leaves crackling as you step on them and even the smells – bonfires usually – and there is something else. The bite in the air that tells you, on some primal level, that winter is definitely just round the corner. Before Bleaklow, I might not have thought that a wild camp on a peak so close to houses and streetlights could ever feel anything but tame, but that trip had changed me somehow, had opened my eyes to the fact that wild-feeling places can exist just about anywhere.

I'd arrived the previous day when it was already dark, passing through the nearby town of Barrowford. It was far too late for me to head up the peak immediately, being neither dressed nor prepared for a night out, so I'd arranged for a stay in a B&B beforehand. I also wanted to get a further handle on the witches' legend before my camp, as well as pick up supplies and scope out the area by daylight first.

The friendly glow from the streetlights back in Barrowford vanished as if someone had magically flipped a switch as I got deeper into the heart of the borough of Pendle. The tarmac under my wheels stretched ahead, twisting and turning with such scary irregularity that I had to squint even with my headlights on full beam to work out which way I should turn the wheel. Suddenly the flash of white from a metal sign reflected back at me. I had reached the town I was heading for – Roughlee. This place was the epicentre for the famous witch trials.

Just then, I saw it – eyes – staring right at me. I slammed my foot on the brakes as her face glowed in my headlights, then all of a sudden she was gone again. I looked in my rear-view mirror to see if I could make out the shape of a person but all I could see behind me was darkness. I continued on. Less than a minute later I pulled over to my hostelry and pushed it to the back of my mind.

The woman who answered the door spoke with a wonderfully friendly Lancashire drawl, making me feel instantly like I had arrived home.

'Long journey was it, love?' she asked as she showed me upstairs to the room, the stairs creaking noisily as she did. 'Bet it was,' she answered just as fast without apparently needing a response. 'Just staying for one night are you?' then, before I could open my mouth, 'I suppose you've got other things to be getting on with. Is everything OK with the room?' – this time I didn't even try to reply – 'I guess you're just happy to be out the car.' She continued this soliloquy for a few more Q&As, in which time I have to admit her answers were pretty much spot on, until she asked a final question: 'Do you know where you're going tomorrow?' She fell silent. Stunned by a space in the conversation I was expected to fill I took a while to form my words.

'Yes... er... no... I... er... know,' I said, and promptly walked into a cupboard.

'The bathroom is that door there, love,' she volunteered politely.

Red-faced, I thanked her and set about sorting out my bag for the next day. The bed was deliciously comfy, but that night I found my sleep was restless; the haunting stare of the woman I saw on the highway kept permeating my thoughts. Eventually after a few hours of broken shut-eye I decided to get up.

Methodically I began to gather my camping kit, packing it into my rucksack. This time all I had with me was a tarp – essentially a sheet of waterproof fabric that I would hold in place with walking poles. All I had to hope for was that the weather would be good, because if there's something

I do know, it's that sleeping under a tarp should only be attempted in dry and non-windy conditions.

Leaving quietly, I left a note of thanks for my friendly landlady and moved my car to a less obvious place. The day was mine to fill before my adventurous night so I headed off to the hamlet of Barley, one step closer to the allegedly haunted hill.

The story of the witches is a truly fascinating one. It all began when, on the lower flanks of Pendle Hill above the village I was now entering, a girl called Alize was begging. She'd asked a pedlar, who by all accounts was quite old, for some pins (an odd request by our standards but apparently not that unusual back in the 1600s). When he refused, she muttered some standard curse at him – the likes of which I've probably uttered a thousand times when I get stuck behind painfully slow walkers on a narrow mountain path. But with what must rate as the worse timing ever, at that exact moment he had a stroke and collapsed, becoming paralysed and losing the ability to speak. Unfortunately medical knowledge was not quite advanced enough to explain this health issue and so – even though he survived – the poor woman got accused of witchcraft. The worst part was, even she believed it was her fault. She began implicating her own family members when questioned and eventually other locals too. The whole thing spiralled out of control and so the witch trials began.

When I arrived, some four hundred years later, there was another furore happening, but on this occasion it had nothing to do with witches, this time it was to do with a burger van, which was apparently threatening the livelihood of the local café where I had stopped to pick up a sandwich.

I left the town and began climbing uphill on a track. It was here that I got my first glimpse of my bed for the night. Pendle Hill rose majestically from the fields below, its hulking mass dwarfing the buildings like a looming giant. Its slopes were a seasonal shade of brown and barley, with great chunks of earthy russet where land had slipped under the frequent rain.

For now, I turned my back on it and made a beeline for the nearby village of Newchurch-in-Pendle, just over the rise from that viewpoint west of the peak. Easier said than done. Though the sun was shining now, the rain from the night before had permeated the grass and I was at the mercy of a farmer's field and allocated right of way, which the kindly agriculturalist had decided would be a perfect spot for his cows. It had been churned up into a mush of sloshy mud and bovine excrement. Even better, the rising temperature in the morning rays was now accentuating the smell of said excrement making this a true treat for the senses as well as the feet. I hopped from what I hoped was one piece of solid ground to the other, misjudging it every few steps and shrieking as my foot sank up to my thighs. A walk that should have taken no more than a couple of minutes actually took nearly half an hour.

What with last night's embarrassing inability to find the right door to the bathroom, I decided to try to find a map or at the very least ask for directions and best routes up the hill. The only shop I could find was a curious place called Witches Galore. It wasn't open, though was going to be in about fifteen minutes. Peering in the windows I saw more witch paraphernalia than you could shake a wand at. Pentagram-encrusted pestle and mortars, mini toy enchantresses, 'witches do it on broomsticks' window stickers, spell books, incense sticks, skull candle holders – all high on the occultists Saturday morning shopping list. On the side of the building, a sawn-off broomstick was attached and Wiccan words carved into a wooden beam above the door.

The sound of what reminded me of chains rattling startled me from my browsing and I looked at the wooden door to see a white-bearded man opening up. I waited patiently while he brought out one of those old 'yes we are open' signs that also advertise the brand of ice cream they stock (we all know how casting magic spells can make one crave a Cornetto), before he disappeared inside. He re-emerged moments later carrying a full-size witch, made from old clothes and papier mâché, who he proceeded to chain to the railings – lest some passer-by should feel the urge to pick up a free witch on their way through.

'Morning,' he said, then, 'do come in.'

I entered the Aladdin's cave of all things witch-like, chuckling at the Pendle Witch black rock candy, gasping in wonder at just how heavy a mini cauldron actually is and staring up at the many hundreds of cuddly toy witches dangling on broomsticks above my head.

Among all this, was something that looked most out of place: an Ordnance Survey map of the area, its scientific-looking, mathematically precise lines and grid system oddly out of place. I picked it up instinctively and was surprised to find it coated with a thick film of dust. Not many walkers must come looking for one here I reasoned. The map behind it was equally encrusted so I took the first one over to the counter to pay.

'It's nearly eight pounds,' the man said to me as he looked at the sticker that read £7.99 on the back and sounding oddly surprised, as if I was asking him for the money.

'I know,' I answered, 'is it OK to pay by card?'

He then did something mystifying yet simultaneously endearing. He said, 'May I suggest a cheaper alternative that's just as good?' Obviously sensing my thrifty streak, he proceeded to fish out a map entitled *Walks in Pendle*. I opened it up with low expectations, anticipating that I would find a sketch map inside, but to my amazement the contours, grids, paths – everything – were all there. It was like an old Ordnance Survey map that you'd find back in the eighties; accurate but with less modern use of colours, but absolutely perfect for my needs.

'Only two-fifty that one,' he said. 'Drawn by a local man who lives near here,' he further explained.

'Oh, he's a character!' came a woman's voice from behind me and I looked in wonder, as what must have been his wife appeared, dressed head to toe in black with a sweep of silvery hair. 'Ordnance Survey tried to sue him you know,' she laughed.

'They lost,' her husband chipped in.

'But they did ask him what measuring tool he had used to compile it seeing as it was so accurate. "Me walking tool, me walking tool," he'd told them,' at this point she raised her leg up and gestured at her foot. '"Them's me bloody walking tool."'

If I hadn't made my mind up whether to buy it before, I had now. An old guy standing up to a huge company and winning – and using just his feet – I was sold.

I left with my map and headed down the road. St Mary's church was my next stop. According to rumour, the witches used its graveyard as a kind of storeroom for spell ingredients. Human bones, teeth and hair were all said to have been pillaged from there and by one in particular called – and this is such a brilliant witch's name – Old Demdike. Grave robbing aside, legend has it that another witch is buried here.

I stepped in through a gate with squeaky hinges.

The sun seeped through the overhanging trees making it look very serene and peaceful. On one side of the church tower was something of an oddity, an eye made of stone, locally referred to as the 'Eye of God' and said to ward off any evil spirits. I paced down the path towards a grave bearing the name 'Nutter', this was the one I was looking for. Alice Nutter, from the village I had stayed in the night before, was one of those executed that local historians believe was stitched up by the magistrate who was leading the witch trials. At the time he managed to get a witness to blame her and others for their involvement in the case. The witness was in a dispute with Alice over land ownership: it was hers and he was trying to take it from her.

There are some that swear blind this is her final resting place, though others rightly argue that the date is too late (1651). Either way, thanks to the very worn engraving on the gravestone of a skull and crossbones (a common symbol back then which related to Christianity and the immortality of Christ, rather than witches or pirates), many make a pilgrimage to see it. I traced my fingers across the impression, thinking just how many years it had been there and how the houses, rolling fields and farms that dominate the view from there, would have changed very little in all that time.

I left the church to follow the road out of the village. Looking at the map I'd just bought, this would allow me to access a field and a public footpath back over towards Pendle Hill. I passed an old quarry used for building the local cottages and walls. This was another aged feature on the landscape, even back when the witches wandered the hills, and local superstition says it was where Old Demdike met the devil in the form of a small boy and offered him her soul.

I detoured to check it out, wary of running into any small children on the way. Thankfully there were none and I walked around its giant slabs from which stone had been sliced off; huge chunks lay on the grassy floor and the whole scene resembled a massive jigsaw puzzle.

'Ruuff! Ruff!' I looked behind me to see a dog bounding in my direction – just my luck that Beelzebub should appear as a dribbling hound. Perhaps he was one of Gwyn's come to get me after I escaped his clutches on Cadair Idris.

'Sorry!' cried a man hot on its heels as he ran over to attach the dog to its lead.

We started talking about the quarry's history and when I relayed to him its association with witches, he seemed surprised.

'Didn't even know it was that old,' he replied, as we said goodbye. Then, as I returned to my quest, I heard, 'The woman who delivers my milk – she's a nutter.' I looked to see the man and his dog catching me up behind. 'And the man who's fixing my door come to think of it – he's a nutter too.'

It took me a few seconds to figure out what on earth he was talking about. 'Come to think of it, the woman in the village up there, I think she's a nutter. And one of my neighbours is a nutter,' he thought for a little bit then added, 'though she married in of course.'

Just then it dawned on me that he was, of course, talking about the surname and its associations with poor accused witch Alice.

'A lot of you then,' I decided to venture.

'Oh yes, we're all a bunch of Nutters here!'

We both laughed as he turned off towards a farm.

'You know that *Most Haunted* came here?' he said as I began to walk away. 'The TV show with Yvette Fielding. Went to my neighbour's farm, said it was haunted. Apparently odd things happened, things moved and all that, then they were convinced that the ghost left the house and ran up to mine.'

He had my attention now. 'Did they find something in your farm?' I asked.

'Did they hell. They knocked on my door and my wife answered. They said: "We have to come in as a ghost has just come into your house".'

'And what did your wife say?' I asked, curiosity piqued.

'She said "f-off!" and slammed the door. We're still waiting to see it air on the out-takes!' I couldn't hold it in, I burst into hysterics and thankfully, he joined in.

Finally saying goodbye and still chuckling a little to myself, I made my way to the footpath. I kept looking behind me every few steps, half expecting to hear his cheering tones again with yet more stories of Nutters. I quickened my pace, Pendle Hill was in sight once again but now I was seeing double. The mirror-like surface of Upper Ogden Reservoir had perfectly reflected its summit, making it rise both above and below my feet. In the now warmer weather, I could make out the figures of several clusters of walkers, sticking up out of its plateaued summit – funnily enough resembling the pins that the woman who had started off the witch hysteria had requested.

Not keen to draw attention to myself – as a lone woman struggling to erect a tarp often does – I decided to lay low in the village for a bit and wait out the three hours before dusk. Whilst there, I did some further research into the legend. It seems that, as with any local legend, there are two opinions on the question of whether or not these women really were witches. Some say they were, citing evidence of mummified cat remains and stolen items from people they supposedly cursed in their homes; whereas others argue that they were just victims of poverty, trying to big up their supernatural prowess to earn money as magic women. With only one biased document surviving from the event (it was written by a clerk of the court to please the anxious king), we'll never know for sure. What we do know is that it happened during a time of mass hysteria when the royals in particular were edgy following the foiled attempt to blow up the Houses of Parliament by one Guy Fawkes.

After passing time with hot meals, bewitching stories and a roaring log fire in the local inn, I watched the window as night began to fall outside. Tearing myself away from the mesmerising flames, I left the town and headed off up the track again, wearing as few layers as I dared in the cold air as I knew I would soon be hot on the uphill climb that still lay ahead.

As the light began to dim, a couple of people passed me heading down the hill, their children excitedly screaming as they enjoyed the feeling of doing something 'naughty' – still playing outside in the early evening. They smiled but I didn't need magic powers to know that they were thinking: 'What is she doing heading up this way so late?'

Minutes later I was climbing the stony path, stopping frequently to admire the scene of streetlights pinging on in the towns below. There were two things I was learning about walking at dusk and beyond it. The first was that no matter how hard you try and how fast you think you are walking, distances will always take longer than the exact same distances do in the daytime hours. The other thing was that suddenly everything looks completely alien. Not just that, but the human brain seems to have a relentless desire to see faces everywhere – even in places where there aren't any. Innocuous sheep by day, look like satanic devil spawn with evil eyes by moonlight, a simple ramshackle wall appears like a crouching troop of armed soldiers, their determined eyes firmly fixed upon you, and a fencepost – don't even get me started – it can be anything from another walker to an suspicious loiterer out to cause trouble. Now that I was getting more accustomed to it, I tried to ignore them all.

A little while later and I was alone, approaching the summit of Lancashire's most haunted Pendle Hill. It wasn't yet completely dark and I was going through the early stages of fighting the urge to start using my headtorch. Though comforting, its white beam instantly ruins your night vision; not to mention the fact that if you're not careful – especially on a hillside like this so close to inhabited towns and villages – some well-meaning person out walking the dog may mistake your constant bobbing around of light as a distress call and before you know it, you round a corner to find a twenty-strong team of willing Mountain Rescue volunteers all out hunting for you.

As I neared the brow of the peak I let out a sigh of relief. Pendle is more of a lump with a flat top, less witch's hat –

more pumpkin, so with the hard work now over I could begin to enjoy the views. From here you can see the Yorkshire Three Peaks – the trio of hills that make up the twenty-four hour challenge that hardened Trig-Toucher types absolutely love. Made up of the shapely Ingleborough, Pen-y-ghent and Whernside, it's a mammoth task to squeeze them all into an epic day, to the point that many who do it don't even remember it happening, least of all what each peak looked like. From here they looked very far apart and I didn't envy the rushed approach one bit. I would sooner sit here all night admiring them from a smaller hill, getting to know their curves and idiosyncrasies, rather than have my whole experience pass by in a blur, merely putting myself through it for a tick on a list. One day I'll get there, I thought as I admired them now, and when I do, I will take my time on each of them.

Stirring me from my thoughts, I heard a distinct buzzing sound growing ever nearer. I looked around expecting to see an insect, though knew it was surely too late for it to be a bee. My hand rose instinctively ready to swat whatever it was, but there was nothing there. Was it coming from above? I looked up, but nothing. It was definitely getting louder. Finally I spotted it: a fan-assisted paraglider, his little parachute spread high above his tiny form as he sped above the distant hills. Then I realised he was coming my way. I watched in awe as he floated towards me, the graceful arch of fabric silhouetted against the darkening sky. He was nearly level with me and I looked up to see him wave before he flew by and sank into the distance, the buzz of his engine becoming soft and hushed. It was nice to know there were other people on their own quests to discover these places in their own unique ways.

After all that excitement, I decided I needed a reward for my efforts and took off my backpack. There's nothing that can give a walker quite as much joy as the feeling of removing a heavy pack. It's as though someone has suddenly pushed a button to simulate zero gravity and you are hit with a feeling of weightlessness and total freedom. Astronaut-like I leaped across the summit to the trig point to let myself know that I had really made it to the top. The sun was low now, but from my elevated position I could see it clearly, a ball of orange – glistening like a giant satsuma – and thin swathes of cloud, appearing black in its shadow, framing it perfectly against the horizon line of Morecombe Bay. This was definitely a moment I wanted to enjoy, so instead of making the most of the available light to try to fathom out my tarp, I took out my camping stove and began to brew up.

It may have been colder camping here now than in summer, but that meant one very appealing thing – no midges at all. It was bliss. Actually able to sit and enjoy every last sip of my warm drink, I decided to make another. Then I made my boil in the bag dinner, taking time to enjoy every hot mouthful and with no running around swiping at flies, I could just enjoy being outdoors in the gradually decreasing light.

Autumn and winter are great for wild camping adventures, with fewer crowds, still stunning landscapes and fly-free nights in which to watch distant streetlights flicker, as they did now, like patches of diamonds on the lower ground.

I even found the light pollution was actually, for my current circumstances, a welcome addition as I unhurriedly began scouting the peat plateau for a good spot to bed down. It wasn't long before I found a place a little off the top that would hide me from view, offer me some shelter and give me a great lookout down onto the world below. This would be perfect.

I rooted around for my tarp and pulled my walking poles off the side of my backpack. A newcomer to these bits of kit, I had put this one up just once before and in the comfort of my garden on a warm and sunny day. Now, by night, with the warmth I'd felt from my walk uphill just about worn off, my hands were starting to feel chapped as I fought to hook up the poles to give the sheet traction. Every time I seemed to get one sorted, the other gave way and the whole thing fell down. I was starting to get a tad annoyed with it. Sighing in frustration, I could see my breath in the moonlight. I struggled for another few minutes before deciding that blowing up my inflatable mattress and taking out my sleeping bag would be time better spent. After another fight with the tarp, I looked at my sleeping bag again and it looked awfully inviting.

Just a few minutes inside to warm up wouldn't hurt I thought, and slipping off my walking shoes, I climbed inside feeling the warmth of the down envelop me immediately. I lay facing out to the villages below, the lights mesmerising as they sparkled ever brighter.

I don't know how long I had been out but I suddenly woke up, very aware of being cold under my back. I opened my eyes to see that I had inadvertently rolled off my sleeping mat and was now lying on the cold hard ground, quite dangerously close to the edge of a ledge. It was one that had seemed a safe enough distance away when I'd scouted this spot, but now was much too close for comfort, definitely more extreme than I had intended this sleep to be. Certainly, if I wanted ledge sleeping I should at least employ a portaledge (a hanging tent system designed for rock climbers). Below my face the ground tumbled sharply away and had I rolled any further, I would most likely have woken up as I bounced back down towards the village of Barley. I sat up fast – well as fast as anyone can when fully zipped up in a sleeping bag – then decided that the best way of moving was by rolling, rather ungraciously, back to my mat.

I looked around. It had become much darker now, even though the streetlamps still blazed brightly in the villages. I thought again about the story that had brought me here in the first place and why this innocuous hill had become a central protagonist in it, the haunted beast lurking above the action. When the accused were found guilty of witchcraft, it is said that they were hanged high on the moors. So of course, the assumption is that it must have been here and that this was the place that the ghosts come back to. But they were actually hanged many miles away in Lancaster. Just another case of the way these local legends are born.

I wriggled out of the sleeping bag and stood up to see if the atmosphere had changed now the light had vanished. Standing up, I could see the jutting block of concrete that was the trig point, its white paint bright against the black backdrop. There was little else that I could make out on the summit itself; it was as though all the life was radiating out in a ring from the bottom of the peak, whilst everything up here was still and unmoving. Except for me, there was nothing. No sheep, no mice, no bats above me. I could sense no bad feeling, no spooky sensations, in fact, it was all quite the opposite, the whole scene felt very serene. I was the only living thing, if you don't count Pendle Hill itself. It was like we were sharing a secret view together and that made me happy.

Climbing into my sleeping bag once more I decided this was a lesson to pay no heed to idle rumours of ghosts and hauntings and, from the warmth of my inflatable mat, I peered over towards civilisation once more, watching the lights lose their brightness as the morning hours began to count down towards sunrise.

A drip of rain was my alarm clock several hours later, landing right on my nose with enough chill to wake me instantly. I opened my eyes. It was quite late, 7.30 a.m. and I hurriedly began to pack away my things, hoping to keep as much dry as possible from the light shower that was now tapping against the cells of the air mattress.

As I packed the last of my bits away, laughing at the sight of my crumpled, unused tarp, I spotted a walker just levelling out at the top of the climb. By the time he reached where I was, it was clear he had seen what I was doing.

'Good sleep was it?' asked the man, eyeing my kit.

'Not bad,' I replied, clipping up the last of my straps and pulling my waterproof jacket on.

'See any witches?' he asked with a knowing smile. I suddenly remembered that it was Halloween and before long, the merry fancy dress party would be descending on the slopes.

'No, none,' I replied, then decided to add, 'well at least not up here...'

'Oh?'

'Yes, I saw one the other night, a woman it was, when I was driving through one of the villages near here.'

'Which one?'

'Roughlee, I believe,' I said, thinking to myself, that will give him something to mull over as I leave this place. But he wasn't looking worried at all. In fact, worse still, he began to smile. Then the smile became a grin, the grin a chuckle and then he erupted into a full on roar of laughter.

'What?' I asked, irritated that he found me so apparently hysterical. 'What is it?'

He held up his hand to me to indicate that I should desist with my questioning until he had managed to regain his composure.

'Oh come on – what is it?' I probed again desperate to work out what I had said that was so amusing.

Eventually he took a breath and said, 'That will be Alice Nutter that will.'

Clearly I'd sighted a regular spooky visitor. 'Have you seen her?' I asked, thinking what a great story this would turn out to be.

'Yes, love, I have. In fact a lot of people have. In fact every person who goes through Roughlee has,' he said again and then erupted into another round of laughter.

'How do you mean?' I persisted, half thinking that perhaps I didn't want to know the answer.

'She's a statue, love! Put in a few weeks ago to commemorate Alice for the four-hundredth-year anniversary.'

'Oh... are you sure?'

His renewed snigger convinced me.

I felt like the only kid in class who admits to still believing in Father Christmas (which I still do as a matter of interest).

The walk down flew by as predicted, compared to my ascent in the dark. I worked my way through the village again, eager to leave before word got around that not only had I walked into a cupboard which I mistook for a bathroom door on my arrival, but also that I'd been spooked by a statue.

As I reached the village centre and saw the crowds of children and teens building up for their annual pilgrimage to the top, dressed in plastic capes and pointy hats, I was glad that Pendle had been the hill where I'd had my first truly tent-free experience. No matter how many people descended on it tonight I knew that not a single one would experience the intimate moment I had shared with it. I would leave them to the ghost stories I used to fear and keep the secret I had of the reality, just between me and the mountain.

CHAPTER EIGHT

THE ORIGINAL WILD SLEEPER

'One night? That's nothing.' My friend Jeremy looked unimpressed as I regaled him with stories of my extreme sleeps so far. 'You've heard of Millican Dalton right?' he continued.

'Who?' I asked, feeling ashamed that I didn't instantly recognise the appellation.

'Millican Dalton. He lived in a cave in the Lake District for most of his life, shunning a London job and home in the process,' he explained, handing me a book about this old wild sleeper. A quick skim through revealed this intriguing character to be so much more than just a lover of sleeping outdoors. He was something of a revolutionary. On quitting the conventional life down south back in the 1930s, this self-styled Professor of Adventure took mixed groups of men and women out climbing, walking and camping – all very taboo at the time (especially the women part). He was a pacifist, teetotal, vegetarian who arguably invented some of the first lightweight kit out there. Looks-wise he sported a long beard and dressed in tramp-like couture, always wearing a Tyrolean hat with a Woodbine cigarette planted firmly between his lips. In his heyday, all this made him something of a celebrity in the Lakeland valley of Borrowdale.

His total lack of care for the subscribed lifestyle of his time, clearly brought on by a love of being close to nature and the way he didn't discriminate against women – encouraging them to lead climbs – made him in my mind, a figurehead for what extreme sleeping should be about and the obvious inspiration for my next wild camp.

The more I read about him, the more I wanted to see the place he used to call home. Jeremy, who I was staying with and who conveniently lives within spitting distance of the Lakes, had told me it was somewhere on Castle Crag in Borrowdale but that it was now under the care of the National Trust who, due to health and safety reasons, asked people not to overnight there. Still, with their renewed support of wild camping (if done responsibly), demonstrated by the raft of volunteer holidays they were running which actually involved the activity, I was determined to check it out in the hope that seeing the home of this fascinating character might somehow further connect me with the way he saw the world.

I love the Lakeland landscape, the rolling fells, the deep pockets of water that radiate from its centre like a giant propeller and the different characters found in each of its naturally formed valleys. It's easy to see why a man who grew up surrounded by the grey, concrete blocks of the English capital would relish the moments he spent in such open country. But at times, nowadays, the Lake District can feel a little bit twee – especially in the summer. Visitors come from all over, en mass, and some of them with no intention of getting out and actually walking. All Hunter wellies and Barbour jackets and little kids with names like Imogen and Oscar who would never think of climbing a tree or peering into a cave in case their designer waterproofs might get dirty. I've often gone there on long walking trips with friends and emerged into one of the Lakeland towns before groups of these people and been regarded as something of a pariah because my walking boots have actually got mud in the tread. Sure these people wear the outdoor brands – The North Face and the Berghaus gilets, perhaps even an Arc'teryx beanie hat – but they never get to be tested in properly harsh conditions, with the exception perhaps of the odd foray down the frozen food aisle in Booths. These indoor dwellers in outdoor clothing are the same people who drive 4x4 vehicles but swerve to avoid puddles in case their alloys get dirty. It was funny to think that a place that can attract these kind of mud-phobics was home to perhaps the most famous wild sleeper there ever was in Britain. The Lakes could certainly use someone like him now to prove that there is adventure beyond the tearooms, B&Bs and Beatrix Potter and perhaps, I say with some modesty, I am the woman for the job!

Picking up an Ordnance Survey map in Ambleside I headed to the nearest coffee shop to begin a hunt for the likely spot of Millican's cave home. It didn't take much searching. There, marked below the contours of Castle Crags peak, was the simple word 'Caves' slapped somewhere between the summit rocks and the footpath that skirts at the bottom of its flanks. I didn't need an X to mark the spot, the treasure had already been found and it slowly dawned on me that I now had to follow through on my quest and go and find it and hopefully spend a night in it.

This threw up two problems. The first was that I would be risking the embarrassment of being found out by the National Trust bods and asked to move on; this, I reasoned, could easily be overcome with a feigning of ignorance. 'What? I can't stay? Oh but I wasn't going to, just lost track of time, sorry – sleeping bag? What sleeping bag? Oh this little thing? No I was just warming myself up for the walk back to the campsite,' was my well-rehearsed excuse. But the second and slightly more troublesome problem was the issue of my fear of caves. I may love the outdoors and camping, but caves are something else entirely – they are the opposite of the landscapes I adore. Rather than wide, open spaces, they are enclosed, dark and imprisoning. I shuddered as I recalled the time in the school holidays when my friend Claire and I decided to venture into one in the hill behind our High Street. We knew from local talk where the network of old quarrying tunnels opened up and decided to take time out to explore them. We never made it any further than the entrance. As we argued at the gaping hole, looking into what seemed like endless darkness, over who should go first, a single bat flew out causing us to run like lunatics shrieking all the way back to town. Though in reality it was the tiniest of winged creatures, by the time we caught the bus back home, it was the size of a giant vampire bat. Once we had walked up the hill to her house, it had followed us for miles and by the time we discussed it again before going to sleep, we were both in agreement that we were lucky to be alive after such a vicious encounter.

I wish my phobia had come from a time when one of us had got caught in a pothole finding a new route, or one of us had fallen down a mineshaft while helping a stranded toddler and had to battle our way back to the surface. It was hardly as dramatic a tale as it could have been, but then these fear-causing experiences rarely are. Either way I swore I would never bother with caves.

As I looked down at my outdoor clothes, which so far looked as squeaky clean as those of the gang of fifty-somethings at the table next to me, I decided to make my getaway lest I too turned into an indoor dweller in all the gear (or before one of them notice my cracked and peeled boots beneath my pristine walking trousers and asked me to leave).

It was time to face my fears head on, especially seeing as I had conquered many already. I had after all, on my travels prior to this adventure, come face-to-face with really big bats, not least the flying foxes that swoop down on unsuspecting tourists checking out the Sydney Opera House. I remember heading out on a date to the Botanical Gardens one night for a romantic picnic beneath the boughs of the trees. As the shape of Australia's landmark was lit by the amber glow of sundown, the colours were stupendous. The atmosphere was electric and the birds flying above me were beautiful and exotic... until my date pointed out that the 'birds' were in fact giant bats. Suddenly the mood was gone. I was distracted by the sound of their wings flapping dangerously close to my head. They were out to get me I was sure, and all I wanted to do was leave. Not wanting to bail on this romantic night I sat it out with an inane grin stuck to my face as I desperately insisted to him, 'I'm alright, don't worry, I love bats.'

If I could survive that, I reasoned as I sat on the bus to Borrowdale skirting the shores of Windermere, then I could certainly cope with one night inside a cave. As I alighted at the head of the valley the driver eyeballed me suspiciously.

'You staying at the hotel?' he asked as I followed behind the last of the passengers – all of whom he appeared to be on first-name terms with.

'In a manner of speaking,' I mysteriously replied in as casual a tone as I could muster. He seemed to shake his head slightly as he swung the doors shut and I panicked that he was now heading off to alert the authorities. Regardless, I began walking further down the road than his bus route ventured, eventually picking up a track that took me level with the hill that hid Millican's cave.

Though small, from the approach the fell looks seriously pointy – like a proper mountain in miniature. Seeing as I could ascend it in no time at all, I decided to head to its summit first, then make my way down from there to find the cave. It didn't take long to reach the top. A well-structured path contoured around its slopes like a slate helter-skelter with handmade towers of stone pointing the way as it went. Something that well-made in Lakeland is a surprise to enjoy without an entrance fee, so I took my time on the final steps, gazing down the valley I'd just travelled from, my back towards the town I'd left behind. I never expected there to be such a stunning panorama. The miles of water stretched like a giant looking glass all the way to Keswick, reflecting the surrounding fells in the mirrored surface. Being late autumn, the higher peaks were coated with a thin dusting of snow, accentuating their height spectacularly. I could have quite happily sat there for hours admiring the vista and had to talk myself out of abandoning my cave search in favour of camping right there on the summit. 'I'm doing this for Millican,' I told myself and reluctantly left the top, this time taking a different route down, off the path and into the treeline.

If you think about the different fairy tales and bedtime stories that were read to you as a child and do a mental count of how many include bad things happening in forests, I guarantee that immediately you can think of at least three. I've done this and can, off the top of my head without even devoting too much time to it, come up with at least five.

Hansel and Gretel go into a deep dark wood, get lost and nearly come to their end at the hands of a cannibalistic witch. Goldilocks heads into the woods, breaks into a house and nearly gets eaten by bears. Little Red Riding Hood goes to see grandma, who happens to live in the woods, and is almost savaged by a wolf. Snow White takes refuge in the enchanted forest, foolishly eats the wrong kind of apple and barely escapes with her life. Finally Rapunzel, imprisoned in a tower by an evil enchantress, finds the man of her dreams but then loses it all and where did this happen? You guessed it... in the middle of the woods.

Whether it's the mystical qualities of old trees, the noticeable temperature drop always experienced when you enter a wooded area, or the amount of wildlife hidden in the forest undergrowth – I don't know, but the fact is, woodland can be pretty forbidding. Even if from the outside it looks fairly innocuous, inside it can suddenly become a labyrinth of paths and possibilities, and getting lost once you leave the well-trodden path is virtually inevitable – breadcrumbs are definitely required. That was a thought I was trying to shake off as I stepped off the familiar trail to feel my way through trees laden with thick blankets of wet moss. I had one navigational hint on my side – I knew that at least I was heading downhill – but other than that, after the first five minutes, I couldn't have pinpointed my location on a map if you had offered me a million pounds.

For a place so sheltered from the elements, it certainly had taken on a lot of water. My feet were already wet from sinking into pockets of murky puddles that from the surface appeared as perfectly amiable pieces of firm grass. Solid-looking trunks of fallen trees broke unexpectedly under foot, and branches I grasped for stability suddenly gave way, sending me flying downwards by several feet. It certainly felt like I was in something of a battle with this landscape and knew that the odds were not in my favour.

After slipping into yet another watery chute, now wetting my bruised backside to add uncalled-for insult to injury, I decided that finding the cave had been relegated to number two on my list of priorities; number one would be getting out of there in one piece. As a slimy lump of mud and lichen welded itself to my palm and I struggled to get back on my feet, I wondered if Millican had ever had to endure such a nightmare journey back home. Perhaps he had done so only after a couple of pots of tea in the nearby hamlet, stumbling back stone-cold sober, but feeling drunk as he tripped over tree roots and being smacked in the face by branches as was happening to me right that minute.

I was shivering with the cold by the time I stumbled upon a track and nearly doubled back in horror. This wasn't just a faint line made by a solitary deer, a natural funnelling in the undergrowth created by woodland dwellers. This was a proper, paid for and pedestrianised by the National Trust, path. Its edges were defined by gravel, and collections of tiny stones lay along it like magic route-finding dust. How could it have been that all my off-the-track exploration had deposited me on such a thoroughfare? I must have overshot my cave. Though it was tempting to abandon my search now that nature had offered me an escape route, I turned my back on the path and headed back into the trees, determined that I would find it.

Minutes later, the man-made markers disappeared and I felt truly lost amid the twisted branches and rotting green foliage once more. My task it seemed had encountered a hitch and, without really know what I was doing, I closed my eyes and span around, stopping when I thought it felt right, then resolutely heading in that direction. It was clearly the action of a desperate and slightly crazy person but remarkably, it worked. Seconds later I found a fainter tracing of a trajectory underfoot and something in my head told me it was right. Then I saw an opening – a cave. Nothing deep and menacing, just a large opening in the rocks. It wasn't it, but I knew I was getting close.

Millican Dalton's abode was famous for being split-level – a kind of penthouse in cave real-estate terms, both upstairs and downstairs accessible by naturally occurring stone steps (all very 'new' Lake District if you think about it). Not knowing if this feature had survived the years during which the cave had lain without an occupier, it was all I had to go on so I was keeping my eyes peeled for it. I headed further up the slopes until a huge slab of rock blocked me from going any further. It felt like I was nearly there and I wasn't going to let this stop me, so I cut around its edge as close to it as I could until I came to a flattened section of ground and, sadly, a couple of discarded beer cans. Someone had been here before and

I was willing to bet Millican hadn't left a stash of crumpled Stella Artois tins here before he went. Suddenly the prospect of a giant bat seemed far preferable to meeting a drunken camper staggering around in a stupor and I hoped this wasn't a sign of a reoccurring visitor. Then, out of the corner of my eye, I spotted it. At first I thought it was just my imagination, but this was too clear. There in the rock, next to a cavernous arch-like crag, were letters carved into one of the walls. I practically ran over to read Millican's self-penned epitaph: 'Don't Waste Words, Jump to Conclusions'.

It was amazing to have heard about this inscription in the days leading up to this trip and to finally see it in all its glory. I had to run my fingers over the words to make sure they weren't just a projection of my over-eager imagination. They felt as fresh as they did when first chiselled into the cave walls. Their presence meant that I was in fact in the upstairs of this rocky apartment, somehow having bypassed the downstairs. I chucked off my backpack and searched around in the lid for my headtorch. Shining it inside, I saw the back wall; this wasn't a scary, deep tunnel cave after all but a fairly shallow natural shelter, big enough to keep the wind and rain at bay, but open enough to prevent a closed-in feeling. I shone the light around and spotted the start of the stairs. Heading inside, where the echoes of the dripping water reverberated from the rock around me, I took the stairs down to the lower floor. Here the cave was easily three times the size, stalactites hanging down, some clusters resembling rocky chandeliers. Millican had boasted many times about how his cave had running water and from down where I was he certainly wasn't wrong, a constant trickle was definitely flowing. The temperature was several degrees cooler than the forest even, and I was thankful I'd brought with me a waterproof sleeping bag and plastic cover.

Heading back upstairs I decided to make camp and began by getting out some candles and nestling them into the nooks in the wall. The tiny orange glows lit up the stone instantly and though the heat they gave was certainly minimal, the warmth they added to the cave's atmosphere was immense. Shadows flickered on the walls as night fell outside. I set up my sleeping bag and climbed in, the heat from it suddenly engulfing me. From there I fired up my stove, listening in awe as the bubbles inside popped loudly courtesy of the stone amplification the cave offered. I'd been worried about the place feeling cold and unfriendly, but was amazed at how somewhere this wild could suddenly feel so homely.

I lay still for a while thinking about the cave's former inhabitant. The spot I'd chosen to spread out my sleeping bag was where Millican used to sleep. It was less sheltered from the elements than the bigger lower level, but certainly felt more like a bedroom. In fact in years gone by, other hardy travellers had attempted to replicate his lifestyle by spending several days there, though in a tent rather than out in the cave itself, and they were, of course, all moved on.

As I patiently waited, convinced that any second, a ranger would come and do the same to me, I noticed a fluttering above. Tiny bats flittered about, darting to and fro in the rafters of the stone house. I thought I would be screaming but actually, from the safety of my sleeping bag, I felt an odd sensation. I was struck by how beautiful this scene was, the flapping sound of the bat wings was almost reassuring, and the way they navigated the uneven rock was like an elaborate stage show with my flickering candles acting as tiny spotlights. Clearly Millican's cave was giving me a glimpse into the way he viewed things and for that I felt eternally grateful. I watched the bats perform an aerial dance and their movements were so hypnotic that I soon found myself fighting to keep my eyes open.

I woke up hours later as the sound of the trickling water invaded my dreams, forcing me awake. I tried to ignore it, squeezing my eyes tighter shut in an attempt to counter it, but to no avail. It was like having a ticking clock in a bedroom – the type that is just too loud to become a rhythmic sound to fall asleep to. Normally in this situation, I'd simply get out of bed and remove the batteries – but this was one tick I couldn't relieve so easily. I opened my eyes. Inside the cave, everything was really dark, the candles having extinguished themselves many hours ago. The walls seemed to give off a constant supply of cold air and I realised that I'd inadvertently taken my hand out from the covers during my sleep and it, along with my nose, were pretty much numb. Through the gap in the cave opening, the blackness appeared as more of a pale grey and in the frosty night I could make out the cloud that my breath formed against the white light from the stars.

I snuggled down further in my sleeping bag, pressing my nose against the down filling to try to warm it up. I must have nodded off again because I woke up suddenly with my nose creased at an uncomfortable angle, struggling to breathe properly. Turning over I felt a chill on the part of my body not resting against the reflective chambers of the sleeping mat and tried rubbing my arms to warm up. The water was louder than ever and I soon realised that it was raining outside too, the pelting droplets were adding to the chords the water trickle was playing, in an ever-increasing cacophony. I had front row tickets to a natural orchestra, the only issue being that I was now in need of an intermission. That's the problem with the sound of flowing water, it can sound delightful but can also act as a diuretic.

I went through the annoying task of unzipping myself from my cosy bed to be hit with the icy chill of a cave. No wonder Millican only stayed there in the summer time, then the rock must have acted more like a storage heater, keeping its warmth well into the small hours. Now it had the opposite effect and I suddenly felt like an ice lolly in my own personal freezer. I headed out as far as I dared, imagining the sheer horror that I'd feel if at that moment, a National Trust worker suddenly appeared.

Squatting down I got a strange feeling, like I was being watched. I turned off my headtorch so as not to be lit up like a hunched-over beacon, and frantically did a visual search of the undergrowth. There were definitely eyes on me somewhere but I couldn't pinpoint where. Of course at night, in the middle of the woods, there were eyes on me – much more than just one set, probably tens if not hundreds – as all the local wildlife wondered what this uncoordinated human was doing in their domain. Business taken care of with no humiliating interruptions, I got up and began feeling my way back to the cave with my light still off. Trying to sneak around as stealthily as I could manage, I stepped backwards. CRACK! I actually jumped. With a rush of relief I realised it was just the sound of me standing on a branch. I took a couple of seconds to try to take in the information that everything was fine and it was just a twig. Then, with my heart still racing, I turned to walk back to my sleeping bag and unwittingly went headfirst into a spider's web.

'ARRGGHH!!!' I cowered in fear, what the hell was that unearthly sound? It was the shriek of a woman about to be murdered I was sure. Then I realised it had actually come out of my mouth. I was wholeheartedly ashamed of myself. I was supposed to be an extreme sleeper extraordinaire, not a hysterical damsel in distress, jumping at my own shadow and even my own scream. Now surely having given my location away to not just the forest dwellers, but also every resident in nearby Borrowdale and Seathwaite, I picked the coarse thread off my face and flicked my hair around, somehow remaining calm regardless of the fact that I was now convinced that a giant tarantula must now be on me.

Heading back to the bed, still a little flushed from my escapade, I had almost forgotten how cold it was in the cave. I climbed back into my sleeping bag and noticed a strange noise filling my head. It was the sound of my own teeth chattering. I couldn't quite believe how many weird sounds I was making – never mind the forest. Not to be outdone by me, almost on cue, a breathy whisper started to echo up from the downstairs of the cave.

'Hello?' I shouted, more confidently this time, having gained a newfound cockiness following the toilet episode. My own greeting bounced back to me a fainter 'hello', repeating it a couple more times in a taunting manner before everything fell silent. Then the whisper started again. At first it was fairly quiet, then it began to morph into an odd sort of muffled scream. It was like something you'd expect to hear on a fairground ghost train. I sat up, listening harder. Though undoubtedly a freaky sound, it was somehow still familiar. It got louder again and seemed to almost end with a dog-like howl. I grabbed my headtorch and crept over to the stairs, wincing as I dislodged a stone and heard it fall down into the echoey chamber below with a loud rattle. Seeing as I'd disturbed whatever it was, I thought I might as well go for broke so I turned on my light and cast its beam below. Looking back up at me was a fox, a vixen, appearing almost grey in the early hour's monochrome light. It was the right time of year for her to be screaming, either because her cubs were beginning to leave her or she was looking for a new mate. For a few seconds we simply stared back at each other, a visual stalemate. She was a stunning creature, elegant and proud, her ears perked on high alert, her tail static and her nose twitching in anticipation. After several minutes, slowly and cautiously she began to turn away, looking back every couple of steps as she padded off into the forest. I backed off up to my bed too, feeling exhilarated from my close encounter.

I tried to rest my eyes several times but soon realised it was pointless; I was alive with excitement knowing that Millican himself must have enjoyed similar encounters with the locals, probably on a daily basis. Instead, I lay facing the fells outside, drifting in and out of consciousness, every so often watching the sun beginning to create a fuzzy light behind them, slowly bathing the landscape in its pale yellow hues. Eventually it was light enough for me to class this as spending the night there and I got out of bed to begin deflating the mat and pack away my sleeping bag – best not to chance getting caught by an early-morning patrol.

From where I sat, the treetops ended at a pleasing height allowing me a glimpse down towards the water. Thanks to the change in weather from when I did my solo camp in Wales, there were no midges to chase me around and I ate my cereal bar and drank my coffee with a true sense of relaxation. It was only when I was outside Millican's cave, and glanced back at where I'd called home for the night, that I spotted a National Trust sign advising people to be aware of falling rocks, not to light fires and certainly not camp. Though the advice was probably sound, the plaque it was on felt like an intrusion and could even act as a beacon alerting people to the fact that the place was there and a potential spot to overnight in. Completely pointless, while at the same time, goading you to try it. The more I scouted out the area around the cave, the more empty bottles, cans and sweet wrappers I found. It was very sad to think of this, a much-loved home to a man for whom nature really was his haven, now littered with the spoils of modern-day convenience. Another example of how telling people not to do something actually seems to have the opposite effect.

I pulled out my rubbish bag and began filling it with as many of the larger pieces of discarded packaging I could find until it was full, hoping that by removing some of the more obvious bits, it might at least stop the area from becoming any worse. I left soon after, taking my time to really look at the trees around me as I went, making note of the animal prints in the mud, mingled with my own footsteps from the day before – like a muddy metaphor. As I reached the well-formed path again that would lead me out to where I could catch the bus back to town, I knew that what I would affectionately call the 'Millican effect' had definitely taken hold. I was now seeing things slightly differently after being witness to this tiny pocket of the wild in Lakeland.

Eager to prolong this feeling, I formed a plan. There was another cave – nothing to do with Millican – in a different valley that I had read reports on. This one was not signposted by the National Trust, was not so low down as to attract as many visitors I thought, and was perfect for a second night of cave sleeping. The truth is that in any landscape in the UK, there are a whole host of caves where it's possible to spend the night. Our world has been carved, cleaved and chopped up by glaciers, wind and rain water over millennia, which have created networks of these cracks and overhangs for those curious enough to explore. My friend Jeremy, who told me about Millican in the first place, had slept in a fair few himself – most not mentioned in any guidebooks or on any internet forums – and I was eager to be able to report back to him that I too had slept in not one but two of these naturally-formed caverns.

Firstly, I had to collect my car from Ambleside and drive round to Brothers Water on the Patterdale side. Still feeling elated from my stay in Millican's Cave Hotel I couldn't resist satisfying my rebellious streak first by stopping in a café frequented by the non-outdoorsy, outdoor-dressed crowds to grab a sandwich and slab of cake. As I walked in, I could see that I'd left a few specks of mud on the tiles to prove my credentials. Childish perhaps (I could have done a better job of cleaning my boots before I went in), but seeing disapproving looks as I left and people spotting yet more mud splats on the back of my legs, gave me a real boost for a second night in the wild. I hoped as I left, that just maybe I had inspired a few of the children to get their shoes dirty too.

Food collected and excitement still bubbling in my stomach I deposited my car near a campsite. The cloud had begun to descend as I started on the path and I was glad that I'd boosted my positive frame of mind as this overcast weather was going to make finding the cave tricky. Its name was Priest's Hole and I amused myself noting that it would take either a prayer or divine intervention to help me find it in these conditions.

As the track cut higher up the fell, the clag increased (the thick fog that lingers around summits and lowers visibility); slices of sunlight occasionally managed to cut through it, revealing glimpses of the green and grey of the grass and rocks, before closing up and hiding everything again. I looked at the map. Though I had something of a climb still to go, I knew I must be close and in clearer conditions would be able to make out the slit that marks the opening from here. Once more, despite my survived night in Borrowdale, I began to fear what sort of size cave this would be. I knew for a fact that bats weren't an issue, but I hoped it wouldn't feel too enclosed.

The problem with this cave was that because it was marked on the smaller scale maps, I did run the slight risk of getting there and finding another explorer already inside. That was the one good thing about the deteriorating conditions – they would keep off a lot of the fair-weather walkers and campers, hopefully meaning that I would get the place to myself. I continued upwards, every time the cloud thinned, peering to the left to make out the flanks of Dove Crag. I was briefly treated to a glimpse of its north face, and spied, at least I thought I spied, a darker lip under a wall of stone. This had to be it. I knew a scramble would be on the cards to reach it, but then I've always been a believer that in the hills, nothing worth having comes easily, and with extreme sleeping I think that saying doubly applies.

The cloud swallowed up the view once more, but I had a bearing fixed, so left the path to begin moving on the rock. It felt cold under my fingertips, but nowhere near as icy as the walls in last night's cave. With each step upwards, I somehow sensed I was getting closer to my goal. Despite the gloom, I could just make out a tracing of previous footfall, the white lines and scrapes on the rock of crampon-clad winter ascenders who had gone before me in full-on snowy conditions.

My backpack was beginning to feel heavy as I searched around each ledge for signs of a dwelling, but all I found were more rocks and sudden drops. Then I saw a flash of red above me. Not a natural colour in this hoary scene, but a proper ready-salted crisp packet red coming down towards me.

'Hello there!' came a cry and I realised that the rubicund flare was a Gore-Tex-clad walker descending towards me.

Clearly someone coming from this direction on the slopes of this particular hill had to have been in Priest's Hole and could be my key to finding it... if I would dare to ask for directions. There's something of an unwritten rule when it comes to asking the way in the hills and that's because there are roughly two schools of thought among walkers. The first, slightly elitist group, think that if you're out there (especially in conditions such as this), then you should damn well know what you're doing and if you don't, then more fool you and why should they try to school you. The second are the much more amenable happy-to-help type who are just so glad you are out enjoying something that they love, that they'll even give you their map if you don't have one so that you can appreciate the experience to the fullest. It's always tricky to know which type you're dealing with so I had to decide on my tack when broaching the question.

'Shocking weather,' I noted as he clambered down to my level, trying to gauge which category he fell into from his reaction.

'Yeah, but would you want to be anywhere else?' he replied, making me think he fell into the 'happy-to-help' variety.

'Been to the cave?' I asked casually as if it was something everyone did all the time and no big deal at all.

'Yep, such a shame though, it's a bit of a mess – so many people coming here who really shouldn't.' Tricky now, he was sounding more like group one.

'Oh, tell me about it – I was at Millican's cave the other day – ended up carrying trash out of it.' I said, temporarily pushing to the back of my mind the fact that my chosen bed sounded like a bomb had hit it, and instead, trying to prove I was not one of those aforementioned mess creators.

'Been to this one before?' he asked. Clearly I wasn't being as subtle as I thought.

'Erm, this one...' I stuttered, feeling as 'all the gear and no idea' as some of the coffee drinkers earlier. I was desperately trying to decide if I should either, not ask for directions – man style – and carry on fumbling around hoping for the best, pretend to have the navigational prowess of Bear Grylls, or just come out with it and ask.

Before I had chance to decide though, he thankfully did it for me.

'Not long now – just about five metres up and around to the left,' he explained, smiling. Before I could really thank him for sparing me the embarrassment of admitting I needed help, he was gone, a flash of red fading into the mist.

I climbed further up and immediately found myself on a faint track. Despite not seeing any further than a few metres in front of me it didn't matter, I could feel my way around the rocks. A few steps later I found it. More of an overhang than a proper cave, this natural shelter had been given a helping hand by man, with small piles of rocks stacked at the bottom edge creating a makeshift wall, giving it more of a true 'cave' structure.

Immediately I could see what he meant about the mess. Two foam mats lay boot-beaten into the dusty ground. Old food packets and cans of tuna lay festering among the rocks and from the far corner I could smell the sharp and unmistakable scent of urine. For some reason, a selfish previous tenant had decided that this camp spot would make a perfect latrine and I was immediately homesick for my cave from the night before. It may have been damp, but at least it was excreta-free.

With the wind beginning to pick up and the cloud closing in even further, I knew the sensible thing to do was stay put and grin and bear it. It felt like I was properly pushing the 'extreme' part of my wild camping at least. All I could be thankful for, I convinced myself as I once more unfolded my sleeping mat and bag, was that the impending rain would soon wash away the smell. It's probably the only time I've camped somewhere hoping for a leak. Once my bed was made – as far away from the toilet end as possible – I was suddenly hit by an urge of domesticity – something that doesn't usually come naturally to me. I picked up the second foam mat and began to sweep the ground, picking up and tossing away the larger stones and filling my redundant stuff sack with the less soiled rubbish. I lifted some of the rocks and moved them to form a more uniform wall, noticing as I did just how gusty the wind had become. It was funny to have such bad weather just centimetres from me, but somehow, in here, it was like watching it all from behind a window. The thick mist outside made the opening seem like the fourth wall, filling in the outside with an overcast screen.

As I made myself a hot chocolate in my now tidier abode, I thought about how a tent in this weather would be bending and contorting in the wind and how using a cave meant that I was staying out longer in the elements that would ordinarily have sent me back to the car. Chewing on a strategically-packed bag of chocolate-coated peanuts and supping my warm drink, I sat in my sleeping bag and pulled out the book that Jeremy had lent me on Millican Dalton. For the next couple of hours I delved further into the life of the cave dweller – not even really noticing the worsening storm outside, in fact feeling like I was snuggled on the settee at home on a Sunday afternoon with the newspaper supplements. I was enraptured by the tales, especially of him and his companion Mabel Barker. She, much like Millican, was something of a radical, leading climbs, pushing the boundaries of social expectations and doing what she wanted to do even when society frowned on it. She quickly became my idol that night, a woman heading out into the wilds answering only to herself. Though I knew I was doing nothing so groundbreaking now, I couldn't help but recall the reactions of friends and family members when I did my first solo camp and the relief and cries of 'well now you've done it, at least it's out of your system and you don't have to do it again', when I safely returned, as though my very survival had been a sheer fluke and my luck would eventually come to an end. Of course what they didn't realise (mainly because I wouldn't tell them and deal with all the questions and hassle that would ensue), was that I certainly hadn't got it out of my system – it had just stirred something in me to do more.

Coming to the end of the book, which sadly was the end of Millican's life too, I learned how, during the winter, the shed he lived in down south when not in the cave, had burned down. He took to camping in a tent, but it proved too much for him and he caught pneumonia, resulting in being hospitalised. Despite all his adventures, his natural shelters, his love of being surrounded by fresh air and wildlife, in the end he died in a nursing home, encased by four brick walls.

It was a tragic end for such a free spirit and my only hope for him was that when he lay there taking his last breaths, he was, in his mind, back in the Lakeland cave he called home, breathing that fresh Cumbrian air, and hearing the bats flying above while the foxes cried below and the sun finally sank down behind the distant fells one last time.

Putting the book away, the dreary colours outside seemed oddly fitting. I shivered a little as the roar of the wind all at once burst back into my book-free consciousness. With my phone battery giving up the ghost I had no idea what time of day it was; it was like being stuck in the seconds between the minutes of a clock face. With nothing else to do, I decided to try to sleep and for the first time – despite all the noise of the elements and the occasional rogue raindrop ricocheting off the stone wall I'd repaired and hitting me in the face – I fell asleep quickly and undisturbed, dreaming of the characters I'd read about, of fireside stories and triumphant climbs.

When I woke hours later, some of the cloud had lifted above my cave, revealing an early morning view out across the hills nearby. I must have been out a while because night-time had certainly come and gone. This was reassuring; I had finally become so comfortable with wild sleeping that I was now dozing more restfully than I often do in the comfort of my bed. I toyed with the idea of heading up to the summit of the mountainside, but peering further outside I realised that the clag still remained, despite being higher now. From my naturally formed window, the view was clear though, the path back down into the valley and my car lay obvious from here and I could take my time planning my descent while I made myself a coffee.

On my way back, as I scrambled down, I saw the familiar shapes of walkers coming up, two curious souls wanting to check out Priest's Hole too.

'Hello there,' I shouted as I approached where they stood.

'Not the best conditions to be out in,' said one of them looking at me then beyond, trying to identify the route I'd come from.

'Yeah, but where else would you rather be?' I replied, realising that these two were in the exact scenario I was in yesterday.

'Been to the cave?' asked the other and taking my cue I began to explain where they could find it. Previously, I too had been guilty of thinking that people who ask directions in the mountains probably have no business being out in them. However, the feeling of satisfaction it brought me, helping those people locate the cave and the look on their faces when they realised that they too could go and check it out, made me realise that all I wanted was for others to enjoy the feelings and thoughts I'd had over the last couple of days.

If following in Millican's (and Mabel's) footsteps had taught me anything, it was that there is something more to be experienced by staying longer in the outdoors than just proving to the world that you can. It's something on a much more personal level: appreciating things in a different light. I could already feel my perspective shifting and it felt good.

As I passed more people on the path down to Patterdale I began to consider where I might head to for my next extreme sleep. Saying hello to the seventh person in little over a kilometre, I decided that I wanted to go somewhere more remote than this. Somewhere less trodden and where civilisation was much further away. Once back in my car I grabbed the road atlas and immediately began scanning each page for the place with the fewest roads, the fewest settlements and therefore the fewest people. At first it seemed impossible, everywhere that started to look promising suddenly revealed an A road, but as I headed even further west through the pages, it no longer seemed such a fruitless task. I began to smile... things were about to get a little wilder...

CHAPTER NINE

WILD ENNERDALE

Looking at the Lake District National Park on the map it's easy to see how it earned its name. From the very centre of the park, giant expanses of water radiate out from it like an enormous fan. This is what makes it beautiful, but it's also what can make parts of it very tricky to access – especially when it comes to its western reaches.

A perfect example of this is the Ennerdale Valley. Right on the far left of the giant blades of lakes, this section of the park can be something of a nightmare to get to. By car it's fiddly and time consuming, adding at least an hour to drive times even after you've reached the National Park boundaries. The roads are twisting and narrow – enough to put some people off – and if you're thinking of accessing it by public transport, forget it. It requires several buses and even then it means alighting several miles away. In fact, the quickest way to reach it is on foot from one of its neighbouring valleys like Borrowdale or Buttermere. It was for this very reason, the obvious inaccessibility, that I knew I had to go there.

Thanks to a project by the landowners (the Forestry Commission, National Trust and United Utilities), there is a long-term plan to rewild the area. It's not a plan to strip it of everything that is non-native, shut the gate and leave it well alone to do what it wants; but one that involves tending the land very subtly and stepping back more each year to allow it to go back to a more natural state. A sort of managed rewilding, helping it find its way before removing the training wheels and letting nature run its own course. I was intrigued by what this could mean in an area as seemingly well-manicured as the Lakes and I felt like I hadn't given it a fair hearing. If Millican Dalton had found his piece of wildness here, I needed to give it more of a go to find mine. Still, I greeted the scene that met me as I rolled up at Bowness car park with mild suspicion.

The fells rise up from the valley in majestic swoops – similar to other valleys here – but the striking difference is the presence of trees, and lots of them. Clumps of conifers greet the visitor, masking the hillsides themselves, which is perhaps another reason why visitor numbers are less here than other valleys in the National Park. They crowd the lower flanks, particularly towards the water's edge, a remnant from World War One when large amounts of wood were needed to produce aircraft – and it needed to grow fast.

I'd hoped that the conifers would be the first thing to go here, but on arrival I saw that they still guarded the entrance like great wooden foot soldiers. My tyres crunched on the gravel as I turned into a parking space and scanned the surrounds. From here a clear track – obviously utilised by 4x4s and trucks for the Forestry Commission – led away into the regimented trees and this felt like a false start, a place not nearly as 'rewilded' as I expected. I slung on my rucksack and began walking towards Ennerdale Water, the lake that sits at the end of the valley. This lake is used as a reservoir, owned by United Utilities and, no matter what the mission statement says, to me a reservoir always has the feel of somewhere very definitely man-made.

I made my way through the trees to reach its east end where I could cross to the south side before turning left into the trees again and access the fells above. For a while, the path was still relatively well-defined, so wanting to get a taste of something decidedly more rugged I made up my mind to divert off it, making my way into the trees. Here, as part of the rewilding process, the rangers encourage you to leave paths wherever possible. Nowhere is out of bounds, they actually want you to unleash your inner explorer and I was glad to take up the invitation. Just footsteps later I was surprised to see that almost any signs of human intervention had vanished. Something of a footpath may well have existed at one time amid these branches, I could just about make out the faint tracing of previous footfall – though it quite easily could have been made by cattle or sheep.

The deeper I headed into the trees, the thicker the forest became. Fallen branches blocked my way, forcing me to take a different route. Deep blankets of foliage that had, over time, become cross-hatched with fallen sticks carpeted the ground, often making the way forward a gamble. CRACK! As I stepped onto a fallen trunk on the edge of one of these mazes of twigs, I heard it begin to give. Suddenly I felt myself go. I slipped into the undergrowth and was spitting leaves seconds later.

My leg hurt, my arm hurt and my back hurt too. Nursing my aching limbs I tried to lift myself up. Although I was clearly off the beaten track, I sullenly hoped this place had more to offer more than this old wood obstacle course. When I finally reached standing position, I looked around and stood for a few minutes listening. The forest was silent other than a distant trickle of a stream coming from somewhere nearby. Brushing off my hands what must have been months' worth – maybe even longer – of decaying leaves and undecipherable slime, I climbed over the fallen tree parts and back onto solid ground with all the elegance of a mountain goat in roller-skates. The sound of the water was definitely close. Looking at the map, the River Liza which feeds the reservoir, should have been nearer to where I was standing. Cupping my hand around my ear I pinpointed the direction I thought it likely to be and began walking towards it.

Before long, I started to pick up something of a more defined thoroughfare. Either side of me the trees seemed to arch over creating a natural corridor. My body was a little bruised from my slip, but spurred on by the sudden

ease of my route I made good headway. The babble of
the river became louder and would soon be in view and I
could feel excitement building in my stomach, beginning to
rise in direct correlation to the volume of the waterway. I
looked down at my feet – the rough path was increasingly
lighter in colour as the trees above me thinned and I was
sure I would soon reach a clearing. Then, without warning,
the path ended abruptly, disappearing down into the River
Liza below.

Part of the rewilding project here is to remove, bit by
bit, man's interference in 'keeping' the place. So the River
Liza, which would once have been tamed and controlled
into flowing where we wanted to allow for footpaths to
weave their legal rights of way through the woodland, is
now allowed to cut its own path and carve the land in the
way that it wants. It was this liberty the river had seized,
that had caused it to rip apart the trail I was following. The
ground disintegrating below my feet, the water free to run
naturally: a strange feeling of satisfaction washed over me. I
felt for the first time that I was beginning to see a glimpse of
the wild that might take hold in the years to come.

I let the river win and cut my way back through the trees
eventually finding myself back on the well-established
forestry track that I'd left earlier. This time though, following
it didn't feel like as much of a chore as before, as I now
knew that somewhere nearby, nature was fighting back.

To get a really good sense of how the valley was breaking
the shackles of conformity I needed to get some height so

I began to search for a gap in the trees that would take me out of them and up onto the fells above.

A few steps along I found one. The first bit was steep although thankfully, after a dry spell, much easier to follow with no strength-sapping mud to pull me back downhill. Clearly rain was not something that the place was short of; green leaves on spindly stems reached out from either side of the pathway, so it felt like trying to pick a way through a dense jungle, putting me in mind of the bracken in Wales back on my first solo camp. As I climbed, the surroundings began to change from thick clusters of evergreens to heather, bracken and eventually open fellside.

Finally, I was above the treeline and now the full extent of the valley's managed rewilding began to take shape. I could make out where the riverbed used to be in its controlled state, versus where it had now decided to flow. The trees, which still looked irritatingly regimented and similar from the ground level, were showing signs of stepping out of the rigid lines forced upon them by man. To me, conifers in the UK will never have the appearance of a wild tree – just because of their long associations with forestry – but it was pleasing to see them less orderly, taking on a more higgledy piggledy fashion.

There were patches of felled trees that had recently been cut down as part of the rewilding project and where they had been sliced, a horrible scar was left on the slopes – the landscape torn up by machines. In other places regeneration was slowly happening; visually it looked less catastrophic and more hopeful and with the recovery process begun, green shoots were beginning to appear.

I began to climb a little higher and could now spot the beautiful larch, beech and oak trees of the further reaches of the lakeshore that had not been visible from the car park. In autumn their colours change, dotting the blocks of green spruce with pleasingly bright shades of yellow, then orange then eventually brown, before appearing as nothing more than silhouettes of naked trunks. They gave the whole place a much needed shot of colour.

I headed higher up the fell. The range above is famous to hillwalkers – though they would recognise it better looking down from their summits, rather than looking up from the bottom of the valley. Among them, they boast the peak known as Pillar and its sidekick Pillar Rock, a towering broken-off buttress favoured among climbers for its great holds and unrivalled views. I know people who have bivvied on the top of it, watching the sunset from their rocky pedestal. Unfortunately, I lacked both the climbing gear and inclination to put myself at that much risk of rolling off the edge of it in my sleep – at least today. I'd decided instead to go for its big brother, Pillar, so that I might gaze down from its dizzying heights on Ennerdale Water to the south and wake up to the sight of the sun slowly creeping up from Great Gable – a hulking lump of a hill that sits proudly at the end of the valley to the east.

Daydreaming about the views, I decided to treat myself to some indulgent thoughts with a hot drink. Taking off my rucksack, I opened the lid and began rooting around inside for my stove to start boiling water whilst gazing over to the fells opposite. Red Pike and High Stile rose up defiantly above the trees, their jagged angles accentuated in the sunlight glowing almost burnt orange. Above me the slopes led up to Windy Gap, the scatterings of scree were sprinkled like rocky hundreds and thousands, while the knife-edge ridge on Steeple looked sharp and exciting. From here it didn't matter that there were trees below because the fells were clearly king.

Just then I heard a sputtering from my stove before it fell silent. I knew it couldn't have boiled the water already so I picked it up and tested the water inside, it was barely lukewarm. I unscrewed the gas canister, shook it and hearing a tiny bit was still left inside, screwed it back on and tried to ignite it. It was no use – the canister was too empty to boil anything.

Once it became abundantly clear that I wasn't going to be able to produce any more gas from the canister, I was faced with a difficult decision. With no gas, I would be unable to boil any more water from a stream or tarn on the mountaintops to purify it and make it safe to drink. I looked at the liquid left in my hydration pack. With the strenuous walk I had planned, I would definitely require more than I had. Continuing uphill to sleep there and walk around the felltops would be impossible – unless I fancied being hit with the horrible feeling of dehydration.

The other problem was that I would not be able to enjoy a warm evening meal. True, it was only a camping meal, a boil in the bag curry, but it still made an evening outdoors so much better. Now I would have the unhappy prospect of cold korma – the thought made my stomach turn – or going without altogether. Of course, I could have called the whole thing off and gone home, but I don't admit defeat that easily. So, with no other viable options, I had to head back downhill feeling rather deflated. Before I left, I stole a moment to gaze back up to Pillar, and there I stood watching the clouds above casting a hypnotic light play on the rocks, highlighting the cracks and knolls in an enthralling sequence. Telling myself that there would always be another time, I resigned myself to a night at a slightly less extreme lowland camp and a meal of unappetising food.

About fifteen minutes later, dusk started to fall and I picked up my pace so that I might find somewhere to camp before the woods fell dark. Once back off the fellside, under the cover of the trees, the light dropped dramatically as though controlled by a giant dimmer switch and for a while, I followed the tracks. At the end of the valley is the most remote Youth Hostel in England. Called Black Sail, it is an old shepherd's hut that sits in one of the best locations in the Lakes. From the windows you can, in comfort, watch the hillsides melt into the night before disappearing completely as you eat a home-cooked meal lit by the glow from an oil-filled lantern. It's a magical place and I swore I would come back to experience it again. Now, however, I wanted to make sure I kept my distance from the hostel, away from the warmth of its lantern glow and duvet-covered beds, away from the conversations with strangers and away from the benches and tables that a sleep indoors brings with it. I had wanted to experience Ennerdale with a wild camp, to see if that was the ingredient needed to make it feel a little more edgy.

I continued on the path, occasionally leaving it for a few steps to peer into the trees if I felt there could be a spot just behind them that would work, trying to block out the idea of a cold spicy meal for tea. Then, at a junction of tracks, I steadfastly headed into the woods, cutting my way through bracken and bush and curving my body through densely-spaced trees. I walked for a while, probably not covering that much ground given the time it took to squeeze through this off-piste section and at last happened upon the perfect place to bed down.

It was not only flat, but perfectly placed in a miniature clearing. Although I had difficulty warming to the trees there, walking among them in the dimming light I started to appreciate again how wild it can feel inside a forest. Branches curve over creating a thick roof above and in just a few steps from the path you can feel quite lost. Woods confuse and disorientate you, simultaneously shelter you and block your view, they cut out the light and let it through when they want; you are completely at their mercy and moving deeper into their cavernous canopy is daunting but also, I realised as I explored this spot, exciting.

As part of the plans for creating a wilder valley, a mix of broadleaf and juniper trees had been planted amongst the spruce. I noticed with glee that in the little clearing I had selected for my sleep, there were tiny shoots of a juniper tree, a less uniform and more wild type of coniferous tree. The slow growing saplings I saw wouldn't make fully-fledged tree status in my lifetime. But the thought pleased me somehow that I could sleep in a place which eventually the trees would reclaim. And yet, even the trees were just fleeting visitors in a valley that is sure to exist after all our lifetimes have ended.

Having briefly forgotten about my gas situation, I began erecting my little lightweight tent, the one from the original solo camp which I now kept in the boot of the car as a spare. I crawled into it and emptied my pack out once more, setting up a little nest inside my home for the night. The air mattress was a welcome bit of comfort under my aching limbs (courtesy of my earlier slip up) and I unrolled the sleeping bag and smiled as the warm feathers began to separate inside the segments, trapping the air beneath them – at least I would be warm tonight. It was at this point that I would normally reward my efforts with a hot drink, but unfortunately this wasn't to be.

After colour coding my kit twice and folding and re-folding my jacket in an effort to distract myself, I decided it was time. I had to at least try to eat the curry. I tore off the wrapper and sliced open the silver packet and the wave of spices suddenly filled my nostrils. I grabbed my Spork. At least it wasn't a dehydrated meal that would need cold water adding to it. Normally when eating a boil in the bag meal, the smell and warmth far outweigh the flavour. But now, experiencing this meal neat, I wasn't entirely convinced I could go through with it. Forget the celebrity programmes where they have to eat odd concoctions of animal innards – this felt far worse. It was time to man up. I shoved the spoon in my mouth and swallowed the curry as quickly as possible. The cold liquid mixed with lumps of vegetable began to trickle down my throat. It wasn't as bad as I thought it would be. I went in for a second mouthful. I struggled to go for a third, the spicy smell and the yellowish mixture somehow losing their appeal very fast. By the time I reached for the fourth spoonful I was forced to admit defeat. I folded away my little challenge in the packet, forced myself to lick the spoon clean and then quickly shoved a chocolate bar into my mouth to try to disguise the flavour. It was like eating spiced chocolate!

As I chomped away on my caramel and cumin mix, having missed out on the hot course that tends to start releasing the sleepy melatonin chemical, I felt far too wide awake to clamber into my sleeping bag so instead, I left my shelter and went on the hunt for some long grass or reeds. I had been on a short bushcraft course a while back and had learned a few tricks on how to improvise kit from nature's bounteous supply of DIY material lying around all over the place. Among the skills I had learned was the ability to light a fire, but surrounded by woodland I refrained from unleashing that bit of wisdom on my environment which was – let's face it – a glorified acreage of kindling.

Shopping in my own outdoor version of B&Q I began walking around through the tree-lined aisles. Along the old riverbed were still some green shoots that would serve well for my first challenge. I pulled at them hard – the professionals do this with a knife but not me – without that core instrument I instead twisted, bent and swore at them which eventually had the desired effect and walked away with a handful of that raw material. I remembered from the class that my tutor set about making a spoon with his reeds. I didn't really need one, but I needed something to do to pass the time, especially as I couldn't distract myself by making another drink. A spoon seemed like a simple design, I was an intelligent woman, so I figured it wouldn't be long before I had crafted my own set of cutlery. It might even turn out, I thought as I began plaiting the grasses with no particular plan, that I was so good at it I could start selling them as Nature's Bounty knives, forks and spoons. I very quickly became lost in this daydream, already directing my own commercials, imagining the displays of this eco-friendly must-have kitchen utensil on the shelves of John Lewis and being invited to talk about my revolutionary product on *This Morning*. Pity then, that I wasn't investing my time and concentration on the very item I was already marketing on live television because when I finally took a break from my high-flying success story to look down at what I had been making, it didn't resemble a spoon at all. In fact, it looked more like a wonky chopstick.

I threw it to one side and sighed. Clearly this wasn't going to be my personal big moneymaker. I grabbed my water bottle; it was empty. I reached over to my rucksack to take a sip from the tube of what was left in my hydration bladder. At first I got a small mouthful out, but then nothing. I rooted around inside the pack and pulled out the whole plastic pouch. A tiny drop remained at the bottom. I was out.

Suddenly I felt really thirsty – in the same way that when you know you can't go to the toilet you immediately want to go; when someone tells you not to look at something you instinctively look, and when you know you physically can't have a drink you need one like never before. I decided to lie down; maybe resting would make my thirst pass. I lay first on my back, then on my front, then facing the tent opening watching the outdoor world get darker. Then I hit upon an idea. My first-aid kit. I always kept a couple of water purification tablets in it just in case.

I leapt into action, going back into my rucksack for about the tenth time that evening in a desperate search. I unzipped the little green pouch with baited breath: there, inside a little glass jar stuffed with cotton wool, was a single iodine tablet.

As far as sterilising water goes, iodine is not the most tasty or even recommended method any more. In fact, they stopped selling it at a lot of outdoor shops a few years ago as some research seemed to suggest it wasn't good for pregnant women. As that didn't apply to me, and the fact that the alternative was to ingest questionable water that might – given the right combination of lurking bacterial or viral nasties – actually go as far as to kill me (or at least make me so ill that only a latrine would be my next option for an extreme sleep), I decided to give it a try. Before I left to look for the river, I cracked a glow stick and hung it in my tent so that I could find it easily on my return amongst the thick darkness of the trees.

I walked down to the river, the way lit by the light of my headtorch and knelt down to fill my bottle, the cold flow felt instantly refreshing on my hand. As I waited for the bottle to fill to capacity, I once again felt a brief pang of disappointment that I'd not managed to live out my aim of sleeping up high that night where I normally like to get starlit and dawn views on my adventures. I had always felt that I'd been something more of a mountain girl than one happy to linger in valleys. Not that I'm a Trig Toucher, eager to get up and get it over with, it's just nice to gaze down on your surroundings and take them in from a higher level. Some people believe that being high on a mountain is spiritual I guess because, quite literally, if you believe in the traditional notion of a deity, you are closer to a God up on a summit than anywhere else on earth. I'm not sure that's the reason I seek out the high points, but my journey so far had really started to challenge my belief that it was the only way to really experience a place.

Here with the mere mortals, the bottle reached capacity and I pulled it out of the river. As I made my way back to the tent it glowed invitingly with the light I had left behind, beckoning me as a candle in the window signals to an adventurer that home is near. Flushed with contentment at this sight, I slipped the tablet into my water bottle and watched as the colour changed from clear to yellow. After the curry this seemed too much to bear but then I had my secret weapon – energy tablets, the kind that athletes use to replenish their body salts and sugars. I'd got one off the cover of a magazine and I'd been meaning to use it but never had. I put it in the bottle and shook it violently. When I opened it again the liquid inside was fizzing as if I'd put in an effervescent Alka-Seltzer, but the smell was now masked (just) by the scent of chemically manufactured raspberries. It was no cold curry, but I forced it down as best I could, feeling instantly better as the water hit the back of my throat and suddenly I could swallow with ease.

With not much else to do now, no real views to look at now the sun had gone down, no cheeky hot chocolate before bed, I climbed into my sleeping bag. Despite not having done the strenuous walk I had envisioned, I felt sleepy and more calm and relaxed than I had felt before on these wild camps. There was no worry about being disturbed – though here I was nearer to civilization altitude-wise – as I was nestled away in the forest where even from the path, I knew the tree trunks would be shading my presence from view. Here in the deep forest I could hear the occasional sound of a leaf falling and brushing past the side of my tent as if the trees themselves were patting me on the head with a paternal seal of approval. The stream murmured to itself in the night and I quickly drifted off into a deep slumber.

A stomping sound woke me early the next morning. Light was already seeping in through the green fabric of my tent despite the trees overhead. I looked over at the water I'd poured into my camping mug. Another stomp and it moved with the vibration. It felt reminiscent of that famous scene from *Jurassic Park*, though perhaps a little less dramatic. STOMP! The steps were getting louder. The ripples from the vibrations more noticeable.

Knowing it couldn't be a dinosaur – though on one hand very excited in case it was – I pulled my arm out of the warmth and comfort of my sleeping bag. The cooler morning air felt sharp on my skin, making the hairs on my forearm stick up instantly. I went for the zip and opened it a little way to try to get a view. Then the metal snagged on the fabric. I tugged at it but that just made it jam further. I began jiggling it about, gaining a couple of millimetres one way, before losing them again moving it the other. I fought the urge to swear loudly. I grabbed either side of the tent door's fabric firmly in my hand and tore them apart. It suddenly went with a dramatic sounding ZUUUP!

I fell backwards with the force of it. Slowly lifting myself up, I peered outside. There in front of me, was a hulking great beast – a very woolly-coated member of the black Galloway Cattle that roam through these parts. These cows – undeniably cute to look at – are another way that Ennerdale is rewilding. Gone are the sheep that tear across the grass like relentless lawnmowers munching and cutting back every bit of greenery in sight; these slow-moving bovines now graze in their place. Their way is much kinder to the undergrowth. They mooch a bit, eat a bit, then mooch on again to the next place and their manure is also good for helping the plants grow. They are fairly shy and I had never really got a glimpse of one before now, but here I was with one only centimetres away from me, munching away on the grass.

I felt honoured. For some it might not offer the excitement of a safari sighting – of a predator coming in for a kill – but for me, it was thrilling. All at once I was glad that I had been forced to sleep on lower ground. Had my gas not run out, had I been able to sleep high, I would have missed this meeting with one of the shy residents of that valley – one who was key to the rewilding that had brought me there. Grabbing my inflatable pillow, I rested it under my chin and there I lay for the several minutes it graced me with its presence, watching it graze, look about, then graze again until finally, the cuddly gentle giant had had its fill and continued on into the trees, its hoofbeats growing evermore distant.

CHAPTER TEN

JURA

'Right hand down!' came the cry and I looked to see the ferry meeting the dock with a clang. A boat ride was necessary to take me to the first of my Scottish sleeps. After Ennerdale, my perceptions of what makes a place feel wild had been challenged and I was hungry to find more in places I wouldn't previously have thought possible. Scotland is an easy place to go wild in. Camping the way I had been doing up to this point was not only legal here but encouraged too. I had imagined I could piece together some really extreme wilderness experiences here with endless days out in the Highlands. First though, I wanted to try something a little different, a sleep in a place that was wild first and foremost because of its distance from the rest of Britain. An island sleep.

It was reading *1984* that made me single out the Isle of Jura as my one sleep away from the mainland. The author is of course George Orwell and the book is a tale of dystopia set in a world in the grips of post-war fallout. In it are phrases and ideas that have permeated as sayings into popular culture, as well the TV shows *Room 101* and *Big Brother*. Of which the latter Orwell wrote, 'is always watching you', prophetic words that bear scary parallels to the world we live in today. All that paranoia, constant surveillance and the Thought Police keeping an eye out for anyone having an unauthorised viewpoint would make you think that to conjure up such a bleak view of the world, he must have penned it in a sprawling city with the early guises of CCTV cameras poised for launch. So I found it surprising that the place where he actually wrote this seminal text was on the Isle of Jura.

For anyone who likes to seek out wilderness, the Scottish islands are something of a Graceland. Not only are their landscapes rough and untamed, shaped by the unforgiving tides and coastal winds and storms, but they are truly isolated, places where you feel physically as well as mentally removed from the rest of society. Though not ridiculously far-flung in geographical terms, Jura is not accessible by plane – as many of the others Scottish islands are. It's not even reached by ferry directly from the mainland. To reach Jura you have to take a second ferry from another island, the Isle of Islay. In winter, it becomes even less accessible and I thought it the kind of place that if you were to scream, not a single person would hear you and that, in my book, made it properly extreme.

I felt the salty breeze in my hair and the occasional unruly splash of water leaping up onto the deck as we moored up.

The trip takes no more than about twenty minutes, but it's this lack of easy access, this extra effort it demands, that – to me at least – makes Jura all the more special.

Moments from the shoreline, the rugged fringes of the island seemed to extend out to pull you close. Its three mountains – the tongue in cheek named Paps of Jura (paps being Gaelic for breasts – the Scots it seems think three is the magic number when it comes to mammaries) – grew closer, the shale and scree adorning them like lacy underwear and the purple heather looked vibrant and glimmering in the light.

I took the local bus that was waiting for us into town. The town – the one and only town on the island – is called Craighouse, but there are villages on the mainland that feel busier. It is a small cluster of cottages and houses gathered around the only pub, the one main road and the village store and post office. It felt very odd, but yet very friendly all at the same time, almost like stepping back to another era. As I walked from the bus stop to the shop to pick up some snacks for my night ahead a car passed me and the driver offered a big cheery wave. I automatically looked behind me, convinced that a local was there who knew him well. I swung around – no one was there but me. I shyly lifted up my arm and gave a tiny wave as he passed by, still less than sure it was me he meant to greet. A few steps on, two people walked past me and struck up a conversation asking me how I was, where I was headed and if they could help me with anything. It was quite bizarre. Like being in *The*

Stepford Wives or something where everyone is robotically nice to everyone else.

Fearful I would encounter yet more shiny, happy strangers I ducked into the local store to escape. The bell rang as the door shut and I spotted two ladies deep in conversation. They stopped and turned to look at me – I half expected the record on the metaphorical jukebox to suddenly scratch to a pause – as I wandered through the baked bean and tinned fruit aisle.

'Good morning,' chirped one and they both beamed warm smiles at me. They launched into a series of heartfelt conversations about my plans, asking me if I'd checked to see what the weather was doing, if they could help me with anything at all and offered me advice on the best walking to be experienced on the little island. This made sense, I thought, as they started to try to ply me with supplies, recommending more than I needed, but then, unexpectedly, they began to swap items to get me cheaper deals. Then the oddest thing happened. The woman who'd been helping me, wished me good day and left, excusing herself as she 'had to get to work' – it turned out she didn't even work there, she was actually just another customer.

Leaving on a high from encountering such genuine and nice people I began walking down the road again. The island is a miniscule 46 kilometres long and only 11 kilometres at its widest point. One main road works its way from the ferry dock in the south-east of the island and weaves its way from there into the town and out of it again for several kilometres before coming to an abrupt end. Anyone who needs to go any further or explore the western side where I was heading has two choices – either on foot, like me, or in a hardy 4x4. The latter is the usual choice of hunting parties. The name Jura is believed to come from the Norse meaning 'Deer Island', on account of the native red species that call the place home. It's the main draw for those who like to spot native species in all their glory, then promptly obliterate them for fun. But then they argue that with a deer population now numbering around 6,500, there's enough to go around, especially in comparison to the human population on the island which is currently less than two hundred. Although, I proudly thought, I had helped boost it to a whopping 201.

Lost in that thought, I saw a young lad on a cycle coming towards me. He was dressed head to toe in a tracksuit and I, dressed in my walking gear, had an idea what was coming my way – a torrent of smart comments or perhaps outright abuse. I braced myself for his words. But he didn't jeer, he didn't swear, he didn't do anything offensive whatsoever. Instead, he smiled and waved. I couldn't believe it. I must have looked an odd sight as I stood there looking at him with the most puzzled expression I've had on my face... ever.

I continued down the road and just as I was recovering from my shock a car coming up behind me stopped and asked if I needed a lift. I was slightly taken aback; this was feeling more and more like *The Twilight Zone* as time went on. I didn't accept the offer – but I did feel like I had to explain that I really was in no rush. He didn't seem concerned or offended, just wished me a good day, remarked on how the weather was good for the time of year and the midge count low, and continued on his way.

It was as if I'd stepped back in time, almost like the 1940s when Orwell visited, a time when everyone spoke and helped out everyone else, where politeness was the order of the day and people were genuinely pleased to see other people. The best thing was that it was pretty obvious that I was heading out to camp there and everybody seemed very happy about it. At the road end a few kilometres ahead, it is totally uninhabited and the options for finding a spot away from the view of a single soul are limited only by your fitness. I truly believe that no one would care if you set up camp and lived there for several months on end – as long as you smiled and waved when you came back into civilisation.

A car was heading towards me and, now initiated into this other world, I instinctively lifted my arm and gave a cheery wave. The driver stared at me oddly. They looked confused and did not wave back. Had I inadvertently offended with some rude gesture? No, the car continued past and I saw a car rental company logo emblazoned on the boot. It was a tourist and clearly they were heading back to the ferry to hurl themselves back into the twenty-first century.

Thankfully I wasn't on the road for very long. A path simply stating 'hill track' pointed me off the tarmac – and just in time I reckoned, as there couldn't have been that much more of it left. The ground was soft and springy under my boots and at first I was disappointed that there was even something that resembled a path at all. I felt too well directed in what I'd hoped would be a wild place and wondered if I might find another corner shop just over the rise. Then I saw them.

My first sight of the Paps from that angle. I had noticed them from the ferry of course, you couldn't miss a trio of giant mammary-like lumps of granite rising up to the heavens encased in their very own heather-clad, silvery, Jean-Paul Gautier-designed boulder holders. I was in luck. Despite the time of year, all of them were in full view with very few clouds in the sky at all. Due to the small landmass, these three hills – which by no means even begin to rival at least several hundred on the mainland in terms of height – looked like giants.

I hurried along the path which had started to peter out. I didn't need it anyway, I now had my goal firmly in sight – this giant trio. The furthest away from me was Beinn an Oir, which means mountain of gold and, in the light as it was now, certainly looked dazzling.

As I neared it, I reached the massive loch that sits at the base of all the Paps. Today it was placid and serene, reflecting each one of those giants perfectly. From the look of the clouds I could rely on the weather sticking around for most of that day, so in no rush at all, I walked down to the water's edge, enjoying the feeling of being the only person for miles around.

The track was slim and snaking and had more signs of being hoof beaten (courtesy of the native deer population) than boot beaten. It forked and looked like it twisted along both sides of the pristine pool. I decided to stay on the left-hand side, where I could easily enjoy the view of the silvery peaks and their reflections.

The ground splashed noisily, holes filled by previous rainstorms revealed themselves as ankle-sucking impressions. I moved closer to the water, the pebbles in the shallow fringe gave me a welcome solid surface to walk on as the water lapped at my soles, diluting the mud on the edge of my boots.

On the opposite end of the loch where I was heading, sat a little tin bothy; a green hut in what must rate as one of the prettiest spots in which to locate an overnight shelter I'd seen. The closer I got, the more it looked oddly well kept amid the wild scenery. With every step I was heading west, but all human life on Jura gathers in the east around or very close to Craighouse. In the west and also further up north where the island looks like it has been nearly ripped into two distinct halves during its geological make-up, it is uninhabited, a true wilderness with no real roads to follow. A place where discovery has to be on foot, yet very few people dare to tread or even camp due to both the absence of paths and the presence of bogs.

When Orwell came to Jura in 1948 to write his book, he called the island 'an extremely un-gettable place' in reference to the faff required to reach it. If it's hard now, it was even trickier then. Add the fact that he based himself in the north in a place called Barnhill, a good 11 kilometres further on than the road end and his phrase is perhaps well founded. It's now possible to rent the place, which is billed as a bit of a tourist attraction. It had been a tempting prospect, but now as I stood with nothing but a little bothy reflected in the loch, I wouldn't have traded locations.

The bothy was actually a fisherman's hut and because of that had its own wooden jetty that stretched out into the water. On either side of it streams trickled by. I edged nearer and peered in through the big windows – someone had clearly designed this to let the views in, rather than keep the outside out and I loved it immediately. I opened the door and saw a table and two chairs with spare ones folded away in the rafters above. By the window it had some basic mod cons in the form of a cooking stove, some rusted pots and pans and some left-over supplies. In the corner, there were two old fishing rods which looked almost antiquated, perhaps even pre-dating the bothy itself. Like most outdoor buildings – and especially those by water – every window had its own spider's web. In a location like this, midges always come out when you're about to watch the beautiful sunset by the water's edge and so these clever arachnids were ready to spring into action using their webs like fishing nets.

I decided that the spot was so idyllic I had to stop for a drink. It would have been easy to sleep there, a perfect boathouse to make home in, but I wanted to experience things as Orwell did. Even though he'd opted for the four walls of a building when he arrived, he had TB and had believed that fresh air would be a cure (in fact it probably made him worse more quickly, and eventually killed him); so he opted to sleep outside in an old army tent instead to be much closer to the island's wilderness – and I wanted to do the same.

In the meantime, I rummaged in my pack for a tea bag and my stove. I had visions of dangling my feet off the edge of the jetty into the water whilst waiting for the stove to boil, but as I stepped out onto the planking, I found it to be covered in chicken wire and uncomfortable to sit on. However, to the side of the bothy was a rowing boat – the perfect alternative.

I gingerly put one foot into the boat and immediately felt it wobble. Carefully placing my other foot in, I quickly grabbed hold of the seat with both hands to stop from tumbling straight back out the other side. I plonked myself down clumsily waiting for the rocking to subside. It was then that I realised I'd left my water bottle on the jetty. Not wanting to go through the balancing act again I had a brainwave – I would use the lake water. With the stream trickling into it fairly fast, as long as the water was boiled, I would be fine.

I leaned over the side of the boat and submerged my cup thinking how great I was at concocting such a well-devised plan. Unfortunately, I came back up too quickly and my unstable vessel rocked so violently back to the other side that it flung all the water I'd collected in my mug, up into the air, which then landed all over me. I couldn't believe it – I was soaked. How so much water could come out of one mug is, I believe, one of life's greatest mysteries. I would have probably stayed drier if I'd jumped in the lake.

Not only that, but as I leaned down again to retrieve more stream water and began to boil it, pleased that at least everything would dry quickly in the sunny weather, I realised that my sunglasses had come off my head. They were lying broken on the bottom of the boat with one of the lenses sitting several centimetres from the frame. What a disaster. The sound of bubbling water alerted me to the fact that I could at least enjoy my hard-fought for brew so I made it quickly hoping I wouldn't have any more accidents in the process.

As I sat there supping my drink in complete silence I imagined, not for the first time on this journey, what a sight I must appear to any onlookers, drifting in a boat covered in water, looking like I'd been caught in a raging sea storm and then marooned on this tiny island for several weeks. It only needed the final touch of putting on my broken sunglasses – complete with one lens – and the seamless transition into full-on pirate would be complete.

Just then I thought I saw movement on the mountain slopes above. Scanning the clusters of jagged rocks, purple heather and clumps of moss I tried to pick up what it was that was moving. It was as if the landscape itself had come alive. Then I realised, it was deer. The locals were all coming to take a look at me, the newcomer to their island. At first

I only spotted one, by its tail – a shot of white fur amid a warm auburn-chestnut coat. From spying that, I could make out its neck, then head, some small antlers above and finally its eyes transfixed on me, as mine were on it. Neither of us dared to move. Then I spotted the second one, only a few steps away from the first, another pair of eyes looking right at me. This one looked like it had a strange growth emerging from its behind – then I realised the 'growth' was the head of another deer behind it, its fur blending into the colours of the hillside. I looked to the left of them and there was another, then another – and another. Suddenly, like one of those Magic Eye pictures back in the mid-nineties (where a series of coloured dots would 'hide' an image that you had to sit and stare at for hours to train your eyes how to see it), the picture within the bigger landscape emerged in glorious 3D. A whole herd of deer were on the slopes of the most inland Pap – all looking right at me.

And there we were, in a kind of man versus mammal staring contest, neither wanting to be the first to look away. I felt like I was in a trance and the funny thing was I wasn't in any hurry to get out of it. The sun warmed my face, the hot drink cupped in my hands made me feel all cosy and snug and the gracious animals emerging from the stunning mountainscape looked like an elaborate tapestry.

Suddenly our game was disturbed. Something higher up the hill dislodged a pocket of scree and small stones sending them sliding down, coughing up a powdery dust – the deer were spooked. One by one they looked about them as if asking the others what they should do, then one started to run and that was all it took. Being pack animals if one goes they all go and they began to disappear over the col between the two peaks, no doubt heading further north, away from the multi-coloured stranger who made them so uneasy.

This felt like a cue for me to make a move too – and yet I was so happy to be sitting there, languidly listening to the water lapping against my boat, it was easy to see how time would slip away without you even noticing. I tilted my head back and rested it on the stern of the boat, thinking about enjoying my extreme sleep right there after all, although not sure it would really count. Then I caught site of the summit of Beinn an Oir from out of the corner of my eye and it looked perfect, not even a cloud in sight and the views from the top – surely they would be amazing.

Resolutely I heaved myself up and carefully stepped out of the boat on the shoreline side straight into the shallowest part of the loch hoping the splashing of the water and urgency of getting to dry land would spur my lazy legs into action. It worked. Minutes later I had stashed away my equipment, stowed my broken sunglasses in the side pocket of my rucksack and was on my way, following the deer, to the mountain's col.

It was steeper than it had looked from my relaxed position, and the long grass hid jagged stones that were hard to make out from above, causing me to stumble more than a couple of times. I wouldn't let it stop me. This was the wilderness I had come for, this absence of clear tracks was why I stood here now, there was no way I could hate it for the very reason I had singled it out. It was hard though to explain this reasoning to my legs and for the first ten minutes of the climb, they protested violently with spasms and twangs of pain. I soldiered on stomping through mud, occasionally stubbing my toe on an ill-placed rock until finally the slope began to flatten and I reached the col, tired but happy. There was no sign of the skittish deer up there, they must have been long gone, but from there I could see just how far they might venture. The second Pap now stretched up in majestic fashion all pointed and adorned by scree that seemed to glisten like a precious metal in the light. From that point, the land stretched north to even wilder areas of the island. Part of me wanted to just keep on going in the footsteps of my quadruped pals and venture into the uncharted, well and truly off-piste. Good sense stopped me from actually doing it, but in my mind, I was already lost out there wandering the landscape like a gothic heroine of windswept moors – perhaps in a long flowing dress – resembling a pre-Raphaelite painting.

It was all very beautiful, but of course completely imaginary, and with that thought disappearing into the wilds beyond, I turned sharply left and began to take a faint zigzag line that I could just make out in the scree ahead, heading towards the top. Unlike the usual frustration of walking on stones, where you seem to fall back two steps for every three you take, this was more solid and I found that my climb was remarkably fast. The familiar crunch and clink of the rocks became a reassuring rhythm in my ear as I kept a close eye on my feet, not wanting to slip on the sharp shards. Minutes later I reached a giant boulder – it looked as big as a bungalow and I wouldn't have wanted to be walking there when it had slipped downhill. Thankfully, it seemed stable where it was and I continued to walk on beneath it, until the path disappeared. In front of me now was nothing but scree and if I wanted to gain the summit the way had to be up it.

I put one foot on it and was surprised again to find that it felt pretty solid beneath me. I took the plunge raising the foot that was still safely on solid grass, to join the other one. Suddenly the scree began to slip. If there's one thing I've learned in the years of walking on scree, it's that the best way to deal with it is not to panic. It's a little bit like standing on a slope of snow. If you begin to slip you just dig your heels in and eventually – though granted a little further down than you'd hope to be – you will come to a slow stop.

This is a great theory – and one that definitely works – but telling yourself not to panic when in mid-slide down a very steep mountainside is often easier said than done. I was slipping fast. My hands were desperately trying to grab something solid – but it was no use – anything I picked up would have just been extra weight in my hands. I bent my knees, digging my heels into the rocks, trying to gain purchase. I slipped a little further and then it felt like I was finally slowing down. Grunting now like a tennis player at Wimbledon, I threw my weight down onto the rocks. Slowly, and deliberately, I eased to a stop.

Everything had gone very quiet. I didn't dare move lest I started sliding again. I turned my head slowly to the left, then to the right, then I looked up. Considering how frantic the whole thing had felt, I hadn't actually gone that far at all, in fact I must have slid no more than about 4 metres. But that was enough. I took a deep breath, glad that for now at least, the drama was over. I turned to face the slope and began my ascent again, this time treating the stones like compacted ice, kicking steps into them, driving my toes into the stacks so they connected with enough to form a temporary shelf. Every few steps one of my feet, not having gained quite the grip I needed, began to slip back downhill, but every time, I stayed calm and the slide would gradually stop no more than a few centimetres later. Then I would simply try again.

It all felt quite methodical, calm – Zen even – a term I never thought I'd apply to scree slopes. But in a funny way I was enjoying myself. The concentration needed was all-consuming. Here it was just me and the mountain – it was intense.

Then, almost without me fully grasping how it had happened, I reached the top. The smaller stones morphed into much larger rocks. The slope seemed to have two summits – a lower one, near where I had emerged, and a higher one further to the left. In front of me, the rest of the island opened up in a glorious panorama. The mountain edge dropped away at my feet shooting down to the ground before ending in a heap of scree, grass and boulders. The patchwork of this terrain then seemed to flatten and stretch out for miles beyond, every so often pierced by lochs reflecting the sky like windows in the ground. Loch Tarbet – the giant mass of water that almost rips Jura into two separate parts – glistened as though strewn with crystals, the tiny section of land that keeps the isle as one, looked like merely a thread of green. The northern tip was faded blue-grey in the distance, like a watermark on the skyline. It was breathtaking.

I stood for a full ten minutes soaking up the view until the hairs on my arm prickled as the breeze picked up. I rubbed my skin and tore myself away to head to the true and higher summit. The white stone looked like giant pieces of builder's rubble as I made my way to the trig point. Either side of me Jura slipped away into the Atlantic Ocean. To the west, the flat isle of Colonsay appeared silvery like a fish on a deli counter; to the left of that was Islay, and even further left were the jagged towers and pinnacles of The Cuillins, a proper mountain range on the Isle of Skye.

To take in all these views seemed almost too much – and I could have happily stayed up there drinking them in for days – but the great vantage point came at a price. There was no way that I could pitch my tent up there as I had hoped. With nothing but a mattress of sharp and pointy rocks, my bed would be far too uncomfortable to allow me any shut-eye and the wind – even in mild conditions –

would be too much to bear. I sat for a few more minutes, enjoying this bittersweet vista, knowing I couldn't stay, but longing to all the same. Eventually I took out some food and began making a meal – I might not be able to sleep on that perfect perch, but it didn't mean that I couldn't eat up there.

As the water heated in the stove, I peeped over the edge of the summit again trying to locate a good place to set up camp. Somewhere high enough for good views, but flat enough for a good night's sleep, and low enough that if the weather turned in the night I would find some shelter. I looked down the edge closest to the sea, but it was far too steep. The north was going to be too boggy after the rain and I really didn't fancy a bothy stay on such a perfect evening. So, despite knowing I wouldn't be getting my sea views, I knew where the best place would be.

I savoured every mouthful of my meal, complete with a side helping of tasty views, then began heading back down the way I'd come. The scree was even trickier on the way down, but I felt a renewed confidence now that I knew what to expect. I slipped and slid down the slope gritting my teeth as I felt my body lose control for several seconds, plummeting downhill, before coming to a stop. As soon as I saw the grass I'd passed on the way up, I jumped off the stones and headed for the giant boulder bungalow.

The ground was flat all around this point, offering a perfect sleeping platform. Bit by bit I erected my tent and when I'd finished I took a second to look at the view from my overnight location. From there, though I hadn't realised it when I selected it, I would get my sea view after all – a perfect aspect on the Sound of Jura, the slice of sea between my spot and the Scottish mainland. Beyond that, I could make out the mainland of Argyll and Bute and further away still, I could see the spiky Mourne Mountains rising up from the shores of Northern Ireland. In front of me was the second of the two Paps rising up to match the towering giant I was on, watching over me as I looked back at it. As I gazed at the view I realised that there had been a change in my pace. At the start of all this I might have tried to cram in more mountain summits trying to make my experience more epic. But now I was starting to slow down and appreciate things for the simple pleasures. It was now less about pushing the boundaries and more about enjoying and living in the moment.

I climbed into my sleeping bag and kept the tent flap open watching – as if on cue – the deer returning one by one to the col below. I surveyed their peaceful mooching, idyllically situated against the backdrop of the mountains and the sea, until they continued on their journey while I drifted off on mine.

The next morning I awoke to clag as thick as a blanket. I packed away my things and grabbed a cereal bar for sustenance. Eager to get off the mountain and keep a lasting memory of the previous night's serenity, I began walking down to the col, following the faint path, first to the loch where somewhere in the fog I knew the boat would be bobbing on the surface, then along its edge till I eventually emerged back onto the road.

In the shop it seemed they knew where I'd been and what I'd done, seemingly telling me about it before I could tell them. Then I suddenly understood Orwell's inspiration much better. It hadn't been CCTV that had been watching him. In a small community like this, everyone knows everyone's business, and it seemed that from the red deer on the mountain slopes to the friendly locals in the town – someone had always been watching.

CHAPTER ELEVEN

SHELTER STONE

Turning up at a ski resort before the snow has arrived can feel a bit like showing up at a theme park only to discover all the rides are closed for cleaning – just plain awkward. It was with that feeling that I rolled into Aviemore in the Highlands of Scotland, the base for everything snowy come winter. Its cute alpine chalets, the equipment hire shops, a Swiss-looking hostel, the brightly-lit shop windows boasting goggles and ski jackets all waited expectantly for the onset of a cold snap. Everything here is geared up for the white stuff, so when you see it framed in an autumn glow, without so much as a dusting on the ground, the whole place looks a little melancholy.

But I wasn't here to carve up some fresh powder. Sure, I would be hitting the slopes, but not with a pair of skis clamped to my boots. I had decided to face a kind of cave again; I was going to try a wild sleep in something that could be described as a howff.

A howff is a term used for anything people nestle in for a night outdoors. It can be a rocky overhang, a spot sheltered by tree branches, a crack in the side of a mountain – basically a makeshift bed that doesn't require a tent. They were popular in Scotland back in the day when workers employed in the Highlands couldn't face a long journey home in the evening. Instead they would find a temporary shelter to tuck themselves away from view and the elements. Few people would share the location of theirs lest it be stolen. But there is one that has become famous among walkers (mainly because it's even marked on the map) and that is right here in the Cairngorms: the aptly and simply named 'Shelter Stone'.

To get to it would require a fairly big walk, but this was the place where – legend has it – the oldest mountaineering club in Scotland, the imaginatively named local Cairngorm Club was formed back in 1887 (or 1889 depending whose account you read). The shelter is essentially a giant boulder that some centuries ago cracked off, along with all the other rocky debris that surrounds it, from the peaks above and came to rest on the slopes below an equally distinctive sight known as 'Shelter Stone Crag'. The crag rates as one of the hardest climbs around here and there was no way my abilities were up to the level where I would be able to tackle it. But I still counted myself slightly daring heading as I was for a night under several tons of granite.

I picked up some supplies from town and drove up the road that cuts through the Rothiemurchus Forest, winding up and round the trees to the ski slope and the funicular railway at Cairngorm Mountain. I'd only ever seen it caked in thick snow before, so it was odd to see it still here with all the white ice from my memories melted. The ski lift looked somehow otherworldly now, an alien, artificial contraption all contorted and metallic among the giant mountain slopes. But the slopes themselves in their camouflage uniform – an under colour of khaki green with smudges of well-placed browns and blacks smeared on the top – looked and smelled earthy and rich, a place full of life.

I stepped out of the car and immediately felt an icy chill in the air. The snow might not be here yet, but it was certainly on its way soon. I began my walk up the flanks of the peak called Cairn Gorm – not to be confused (though often is, even by me) with the name of the National Park (which is of course pluralised). You'd think that having given its name to the whole park it would be an impressive beast, but sadly it is not – more of a rounded bump, at least from the angle I was looking at, suited to the skiers and boarders who only know it when it's caked in white.

I trudged up the slope, remembering with fondness the last time I'd come. It was to do my winter walking skills course with an instructor and involved a lot of cutting into snow with my rigid winter boots, learning to do a sort of funny dance-cum-John-Wayne-stagger in a pair of crampons and sliding headfirst down a slope to 'self-arrest'. This is basically a technique where you plunge your axe head into the snow and lean your body against it, and it's designed to help stop you slipping to your death should you be unfortunate enough to, well, slip to your death while out in the mountains in winter. My progress with this was particularly laughable as I had far too much fun sliding and less success stopping myself. When I finally did get the hang of it and bring myself to a full-on brake, proudly lifting my head to look at my instructor for praise, I learned the lesson everyone learns at this juncture: you have to keep facing downhill otherwise you unwittingly allow your body weight to shift, thus loosening the effectiveness of the grip of the metal of your axe and thereby sending you plummeting to your pretend death. Once I finished my course, by which time I had the technique down to an acceptable level, I thought that if I ever fell, the best thing for me to do would be to just enjoy the freefall, because the chances of stopping myself would be minimal.

As I continued higher, the grass became a barren shade of coffee-brown; it was definitely starting to get frosty at night too. The Cairngorms mountain ranges are high, meaning that if the air temperature does drop, snow will definitely fall here. Without any skiers or even walkers at this time of the season, it felt like a bit of an empty place. Magnificent but empty. Around 1814, this area and all over the Highlands, had illegal whisky stills and all across the mountains are criss-cross sections of smugglers' paths – sort of makeshift whisky roads where manufacturers would export their illicit moonshine on ponies and on foot.

It reminded me a little of the stories I'd heard of the people on the Lizard, hiding their loot in caves around the south coast. Here, distilling apparatus was hidden among the heather and on hillsides like this one, near to water sources that bubbled under the dark peat which they used in the distilling process. They say that smoke curling up from the hillside would be a giveaway for the taxman to find them and I'd read a delightful story about a vicar who would play host to the law enforcers, make an excuse to go and tend to his horse, then shoot off out into the glens to raise the alarm. I thought how much I'd love to meet a character like that now, rather than follow the old tourist trail to one of the big-named distilleries, likely one of the legalised few back then, which the highlanders despised.

I kept my eyes peeled as I continued on my way, imagining what it would have been like to happen upon a fully-functioning whisky factory. As I scanned the terrain underfoot, sadly I could see no trace of their prohibited activity, but thought how nice a wee dram would be right at that moment in the increasingly biting breeze – especially as I'd been battling against it for over an hour. I pulled my hood up and over my ears, surprised at what a difference it made in terms of an instant relief and kept my head down as the cool air stung at my eyes and seemed to penetrate up through my nose, making my whole head ache.

I was aiming for the shores of the Loch A'an basin. There were now scores of high mountain peaks popping up and looming either side of me, practically screaming to be climbed, but I was eager to get on and reach my destination. The ground was rough under foot with rocks tripping me every few steps. I realised that it had actually been a lot easier to walk there in thick consolidated snow than it was now. Heading right into the wind and reaching the cairn at point 1,141 metres I decided to boost my dwindling energies with some kind of sugary treat.

I rooted around in my pack and to my delight found a big chunk of Dairy Milk chocolate. Whilst it worked its magic I looked back to where I'd come from. The sun was sitting low in the sky, surrounded by swathes of grey billowing clouds. The thick forest I'd passed on my way up in the car practically dazzled in its evergreen coat. Beyond the trees the landscape seemed to roll off into even more impressive mountains, all looking brooding and bold in the shadows. This place seemed to exist on a very grand scale, bigger than all the places I had been to so far. Here there was a complete mass of razor-sharp edges, boulder-coated summits and hulking giants of mountains which, under a dark sky, stretched out in seemingly endless formation. I fought to remember when I had been somewhere that looked as overwhelmingly massive at this, but I couldn't think of anywhere. If ever I was to use the term 'adventure' with any real authority it would have to be here. Looking around now as a fleeting shaft of light picked out the summits that were even further out than I had realised, I was stunned, and felt a little sad that there wasn't another person with me to enjoy it too.

After boiling some water, I poured the hot liquid into my mug, warming my hands beautifully. I threw in a ginger and lemon teabag and after a couple of minutes of waiting began sipping it with the infusion still in, enjoying the kick that the ginger gave to my taste buds. I instantly began to feel better, warmer on the inside and even without a mirror, I could tell that my cheeks were flushed with a tinge of red.

Quickly clearing everything away – it was too cold to sit for long – I carried on. When I'd done a spot of research about the place, which was even marked on the map, I was surprised to read that some people had struggled to find it. From the photos it looked so obvious I failed to see how this could happen, but I knew in an area like this, out in the middle of nowhere and surrounded by nothing but gigantic rock formations, anything could happen.

I kept my finger (now encased in a thick Gore-Tex glove) on the map where I thought I was, ticking off landmarks as I went. The track began to descend, slowly at first and then down more sharply and needing my hands to steady myself on the steep section, I put the map away. The adjacent stream began to emit more of a rumble as the water tumbled downhill.

Just a few more steps on and below saw my first glimpse of the stretch of water called Loch A'an. It was so long that from my current position I could only see a tiny section of it. Opposite me, I could make out the summit cairn atop of Beinn Mheadhoin, another hulking giant of a mountain. Aside from the cairn all signs of the man-made were now gone, and I plunged down deeper into this glacially-carved valley, the stream following me as I went.

At the bottom the stream split and widened, filled with a mass of stones and boulders. I picked my way across the water, seeing a path on the other side weaving its way off towards the boulder field where I would find the fabled Shelter Stone.

As I made my way along the track, I began to catch sight of the cluster of rocks in which the overnight shelter lies. Among the sizeable few, I spotted one that was a giant even amongst them, and I could make out a stack of stones on the top of it, a mini cairn. It had to be it.

The ground was slippery as I continued onwards, still fairly high above the loch. Mentally I had never felt so alert. The scenery was better than I remembered, with every rock, every summit and even every rolling flank of the lower hills in the distance emitting a grandiose aura that made my quest feel somehow heroic. When a handful of rocks slipped beneath my boots it made me feel like more of an adventurer as I needed to take out my walking poles. Normally poles are something I save as a treat at the end of an epic multi-dayer but now I felt I needed them to give me some kind of stability. This only served to add to my delusions of this being a great escapade – even tripping over one of said poles couldn't serve to shake the feeling from me. I was loving it.

Finally, I emerged at the edge of the water and a beach of golden sand no more than a few metres in both length and width curved around its tip. It looked idyllic. I walked onto it to stare down at the patch of water and look out to the other end of the valley. Bound in on every side by some kind of obstacle – be it high mountains or just a long, complicated walk-in – this little beach felt clandestine and special, a place where only a privileged few would ever tread. I sat there for a few minutes in silent reverie, not minding how cold the breeze was on my face as it whipped across the top of the water. All I could hear were the persistent waves on the loch as I stared around in this hallway of peaks.

Tiny droplets of rain dripped on my nose and reminded me why I'd gone there. I looked up at the moody skies, the clouds swirling in glorious watercolour grey, the whole scene framed by a brooding outline of towering clouds on their way. I left my beach, my little patch of sandy wilderness and set about finding my rock-covered bed.

I crossed the loch's inlet and dared to lift my head to scan the scene again for the stone. The rain was hammering down now and it felt icy through my waterproof jacket. I should have stopped to put on my storm trousers but I was too eager now to get to what I had come all this way for. Singling out my target I made a beeline for the enormous granite boulder on the lower mountain slopes – this had to be it. As I neared it, I began to slow down. You never know what might be under a rock. I suppose it comes from being a kid and picking up stones in the garden, finding underneath a vast colony of creepy crawlies with more varieties than your naive age would have lead you to believe existed. Though I wasn't lifting this one up, I still had the same apprehension about what I might find lurking under it.

The Shelter Stone is more than just a boulder. It's a boulder that's resting on top of other smaller boulders creating a sunken chamber beneath it. Sleeping here is technically sleeping under a giant, person-crushing rock. Over the years, visitors have clearly worked hard to make this howff more watertight and a type of dry stone wall has been built up all around its edges, filling in gaps where the other boulders don't. At the entrance, thanks to careful nurturing, it actually resembles a door at which I knelt down and peered into. It was dark, I couldn't see a thing, my eyes too well adjusted to the daylight regardless of the fact it was fairly dull. I desperately wanted to find the headtorch in my bag first, but with the wind howling now and the rain becoming almost sheet-thick I had no choice but to go in and hope for the best.

Just inside the small entrance I crouched where I was for a minute willing my eyes to adjust to the darkness. I could just about make out a small tripod-like stool that someone had left behind along with a copy of Q magazine. Searching blindly in my rucksack I located what I was looking for, stretched the headband round my scalp and flipped on the switch to create a mottled, fuzzy glimmer of LED. I turned round and jumped as a moth flew directly at my face – clearly pleasantly surprised by the sudden illumination – as it flapped it away. I took a deep breath, it was time to calm down. The Shelter Stone was empty. I was alone.

Peering around, taking my time to shine my light on every section of the shelter, I was struck by how much bigger it was than I'd imagined. I'd say that comfortably it would have slept four friends, and in a real emergency perhaps six, though I would not like to be the one furthest from the entrance – especially if I'd shared a few whiskies with my fellow cave dwellers the same night. Height-wise it was not as closed in as I'd thought, at least not near the entrance side of things where I'd already decided to sleep, rather than being close to the rocky ceiling wedged in at the back.

On the ground, which was dark and a little bit damp, were the remains of old groundsheets, and in the corner there was a stack of cardboard, arranged like a mini alcove for a fire. Quite why anyone would come to a small hole like this, where escape routes are limited and decide it was an ideal place to build a smoky fire is beyond me. It must be for those hardier souls who find the mere idea of just sleeping under a mass of rock not enough of an adventure; they need to up the adrenaline factor by dropping in the possibility of carbon monoxide poisoning into the mix.

I have met these sorts of people before and they are best avoided. Macho Story-Toppers I call them. No matter what you've done, they've done it bigger, better and more deadlier than you. It's guaranteed I'll find one in the pub who, when I mention I've slept in the Shelter Stone in a driving storm, will coolly reveal that when they slept there it was actually a snow storm, −20°C and their shelter stone was one they actually had to fashion out of a small boulder using only their teeth – and did they mention that on their way out they rescued a lost school party and were going to be made honorary member of the Mountaineering Council of Scotland? Those people are out there I promise.

I was amazed at how much of the outdoor elements this little stone cocoon seemed to block out. Every now and again, I would feel a stiff breeze come whistling through one of the tiny gaps, but other than that, I was truly sheltered there. I moved over to the entrance and peered outside – there was nothing to see but falling rain. I wasn't convinced how well I would be able to sleep with the rock just above me; of all the sleeps so far – including the first one along with the abject terror inspired by the killer sheep – this one made me the most nervous.

After unfurling my kit, I went back over to the small stool and found a Tupperware box. I rummaged through the contents inside, discovering a log book for people to record their stays, a couple of broken pens, which sadly made the last item redundant for me, and a few snacks in the form of a cereal bar and a handful of raisins that some thoughtful previous visitors had left behind. I may not have been able to write in the book but, I thought happily, that didn't mean that I wouldn't be able to read it later.

Satisfied that I'd literally left no stone unturned, I poked my head out of the entrance once more hoping that perhaps the weather was easing enough so that I might be able to watch the sunset, but it was hopeless. As soon as I reached fresh air, my face was immediately splattered with a torrent of rain – it was getting heavier. I hoped for one fleeting terror-filled second that the rain wouldn't cause the pile of weathered stones to come rushing down like a rocky avalanche and tip over the big rock once and for all with me underneath it.

These kinds of thoughts are odd, believing that something that has survived hundreds of years without moving, should suddenly give up the ghost just for you. I once visited a rock wedged in a crack between two mountains in Norway and for thousands of years it has been there, stubbornly lingering, happy in its position. But when friends suggested I perched on top of it, I was convinced that it would be that moment when it decided to fall. In the old photographs I'd seen of this Cairngorm Shelter Stone, or Clach Dhion to give it its proper Scottish name, it looked to be positioned in exactly the same way that it was now. This was something I tried to remind myself of as I sat there staring up at its all too solid ceiling, spotting the scratches where a visitor had obviously tried to record his or her visit with an impromptu carving.

Eager to bring some warmth to my little home, I located some candles and placed them at points around the chamber, lighting them one by one and smiling as the little orange glows fizzed and spattered. Then I went back for my stove and set it on to boil as close to the entrance as I could. While the weather was blowing a hoolie outside, rain falling horizontally and even upwards in some cases, my little candle-lit shelter seemed suddenly very comfortable and for the first time since arriving, I began to relax. It could be worse I thought, it could be thundering, in which case I would have to leave the rock and get to a lower non-conductive surface. I tried not to think about the story of the man on the Mourne Mountains in Northern Ireland who hid from a storm in a stone shelter and was killed when it was struck. My water began to boil and my mind was soon more happily engaged in mixing hot chocolate and pouring hot water on to my dehydrated pasta meal.

I supped at the warm drink and turned off my headtorch so I could gaze out at the mizzle beyond. If I squinted my eyes I could just about make out where Loch A'an began, though part of me thought I might be imagining it. I dug into my pasta and began to feel more optimistic about things. Here I was, in a remote and wild valley, with a shelter all to myself that just happened to be the sturdiest structure for miles around, in a storm that would otherwise have turned my little bivvy into a sopping wet bin bag. I had a lot to be happy about.

After a while I realised I was shivering. Crawling into my sleeping bag, I felt my body start to defrost. I may have felt a little bit like a bug with a rock hanging above me toying with my life, but I was warm and dry with a belly full of food. I lay there watching the candle flicker, waiting for my eyelids to feel heavy. At the entrance, gusts of wind would, every so often, blow some of the rain inside, forming a small puddle near my feet. I watched it growing as more and more drops blew in and hoped the rain would stop; but other than hope I was well and truly stuck between a rock and a hard place.

All at once I wished I had someone to share this moment with, another person to talk to, to pass the time with and to join me in seeing just how great an adventure could be had in the UK. I hadn't craved company before, but I felt like I'd reached the point where I could actually impart some of my wisdom, perhaps transform someone else into an extreme sleeper, thereby (I modestly imagined) kick-starting a movement that might inspire a generation. I made a mental note to myself that before my journey was over, I would do this.

I must have drifted off at some point after that thought. A sudden gust of wind that splurted yet more water into the expanding pool woke me up with a start. I sat bolt upright, narrowly avoiding smacking my head on the rock above me. The rain was still falling hard and the wind seemed to have got worse. I peered out towards the blackened night, but couldn't see a thing. Even when I shone my headtorch out at it, the rays simply seemed to bounce back off the falling rain, revealing nothing.

If someone was out in the valley now I thought, I had a comforting feeling that I would be nowhere to be seen. I had become one with the wild I had sought to discover. From the outside at least, we now seamlessly blended together. Not a soul knew where I was and I could have been anywhere.

Resting my eyes, I listened to the pouring rain and felt oddly at peace. I drifted in and out of sleep, occasionally looking to check on the rising water. Eventually a while later, I opened my eyes again and realised I could see light outside. It wasn't sunny, but night was over. The rain was still coming down, but not as heavy as the night before.

Before I packed away my things to head back to civilisation, I picked up the Shelter Stone's logbook and took a few minutes to flick through the pages. In it were a mixture of other people's stories – from those who had stumbled on the place by mistake, to climbers who had planned a night here and those who had just nipped in during the day to pay it a visit. Though I had no pen to record my story I thought about what I might write in it. After deliberating for several minutes while packing away my kit I decided and promised myself that on a return visit, should I get the chance again, I would definitely bring a pen. It needed no elaborate phrasing, no big words or metaphors. I would quite simply say: Shelter Stone camp: this place rocks.

CHAPTER TWELVE

FINDING FISHERFIELD

Now there are times when a girl likes to be alone, but I had decided on my next extreme sleep, that if ever I was going to take company with me, a visit to Fisherfield, in Wester Ross, would be the place to do it. This remote tract of glacially-scoured peaks and glens brings a whole new meaning to the term 'wild'. It's home to the most remote Munro which is a mountain over 914 metres (or 3,000 feet in old terms) in the country, meaning it's the furthest hill of any great size more than 11 kilometres from a road. To walk across the area taking in this mighty mountain takes a minimum of three days, two if you rush it, and for accommodation, you have two choices. Either carry it with you on your back tortoise-style (i.e. a tent) or utilise one of the abandoned and very rudimentary farm buildings and bothies that are left unlocked for walkers to sleep in.

Eager to share my passion for these extreme sleeps and all my hard-won knowledge and confidence too, I had persuaded my friend Georgina to come along. As she's a nurse, I figured if the worse did happen at a place so remote, at least we would have a qualified medic to hand.

'How's that going to help me if I get injured?' she asked.

I just cleverly deflected this with a well-timed laugh.

'So how remote are we talking?' she asked as we left Inverness and she glanced at the satnav.

'Well, put it this way,' I ventured, 'when we reach Kinlochewe and dump our bags at the bunkhouse, it will still take us an hour and a half to drive round to Dundonnell where I've arranged to meet the taxi driver. The taxi driver will then take us back to Kinlochewe, where we spend the night, then the following day we head out into the mountains on foot. We'll be out for three days and two nights and then we'll come back to pick up the car again and – voila – we finish!'

She looked at me for a few seconds, checking for any signs that I was joking, then slumped back in her seat. Perhaps I hadn't sold it quite as well as I thought.

'So an hour or so to go to meet the taxi, then another hour plus back before we even eat any food?' she asked feeling on the back seat for a packet of crisps.

'I'm afraid so,' I asserted, stealing the Wotsits from her hands. 'Be worth it though,' I mumbled as I crunched the orange nuggets and they fizzed on my tongue.

'Let's just hope so,' she agreed and closed her eyes.

Two hours of caravan trailing, dodgy overtaking and pedestrian yelling later (those single lane roads have a knack of transforming me into a less tolerant female version of Jeremy Clarkson) and we arrived in the hamlet of Kinlochewe, which I believe I'm 100 per cent accurate in saying is truly a one-horse town. I almost expected a clump of tumbleweed to bounce across the tarmac as I approached the bunkhouse. But there was no time to explore. A quick check-in and gear dump saw us on the road once more, weaving along the edges of Loch Maree and undulating along the coast. Here the views are spectacular. After escaping the landlocked roads to actually access the coast, suddenly, it's sea, sand and Scottish hospitality all the way. With inlets and islands, rocky headlands and white beaches, lighthouses and little paddle boats and even exotic tropical gardens and vegetation-rich inland hillocks, you could spend days alone exploring this spectacular coastline. Georgina asked if we could stop for photos and I promised her we would on the way back. When we arrived at a fairly unexciting and non-descript lay-by, the taxi was already waiting.

'Make sure you get everything,' I said as she opened the boot to give it one final check. It was Thursday evening and we wouldn't be back at the car again until Saturday.

'So, you're walking all the way over?' asked the cabbie as he wound the car back round the twists and turns of the coast road.

'Uh-huh – all the way,' I confirmed.

'It's a long way,' he said, unconvinced. 'Not any real escape routes. There's a nice walk here by a waterfall,' he suggested, gesturing at the slopes that disappeared above the side of the road and Georgina looked wistfully first up at this easier excursion and then at me. All at once, I was glad we had left the car, it forced us to commit to the planned route with no going back and no wimping out. It was a case of go big or go home and I knew which way we would go.

'You'll never guess who I had in my car the other week,' the cabbie started on a story that I couldn't quite follow but it involved Martin Kemp, deer, guns and whisky. It seems that even in the far reaches of Scotland some things never change.

Back at the bunkhouse it was a case of get fed and get to bed as we had an early start. The next morning began with the ominous tap-tap of rain on the windows. I got out of bed to see Georgina desperately trying to fit three days' worth of supplies in what was clearly a daypack.

'What are you doing? Where's your bigger pack?' I asked, suddenly wishing I'd had the foresight to check her kit before we left rather than trusting her to make the right decisions on her own.

'This was lighter and a better colour,' she replied as if somehow the shade of purple she'd selected made up for the complete lack of space inside.

'Of course it's lighter,' I screamed incredulously, 'it's only 35 litres!' She looked at me blankly as if I was talking in a foreign tongue. It was then I realised I was going to pay for this mistake and resignedly began stuffing her supplies into my 60-litre bag.

'Looks miserable out there,' she said ignoring my selfless gesture and handing me a full-size pillow to take. I bit my tongue and threw it sneakily to one side so she wouldn't notice. I thought desperately for something I could say to distract her.

'Breakfast should be good,' I tried, perhaps a little too chirpily – especially when all I was referring to was a bowl of porridge – but we grabbed our bags and made our way down regardless.

The rustle of our waterproofs provided our soundtrack for the first few hundred metres of the walk, the rain relentlessly hammering down as we began our venture. We knuckled down without speaking until a mix-up over the right of way had us confused. With the bunkhouse still in sight, houses in front of us and another 30-plus kilometres ahead, this had the potential to be a long day.

'Which way is it?' asked Georgina as I realised I was searching for the village on the wrong side of the map. Wild walking may be a challenge for most, but it's the getting out of civilisation that always gets me. Crags and rocks I could handle all right, but throw houses and driveways into the mix and my navigation goes to pot. After a few attempts we were back on track and heading east, finally putting distance underfoot. Despite looking long but flat on the map, the route was turning out to be an undulating ridge via a mix of bogs, slippery moss-covered rocks and towering forests of bracken.

'For Christ's sake!' I screamed – for what must have been the twentieth time – as the branch that Georgina had pushed out of the way so she could get through snapped back in whip-like fashion to slap me in the face. To add insult to injury, I now had a growing colony of midges circling overhead. I was lathered in repellent but that didn't stop a cocky one from every so often sneaking down to try his luck on the parts of my face where some had evidently melted off. Waterproofs were long relegated into backpacks; in the thick undergrowth the humidity was rising with each step.

'Arrghh! These stupid branches,' I screamed again, with another mouthful of leaves. Georgina demanded we stop.

'We've still a long way though,' I argued. But she resolutely sat on a rock and threatened to take a photo of my bite-ridden face if I didn't cooperate. My arms itched infuriatingly while I forced a cereal bar down, as insects seemed determined to use me as a rest stop.

After a good dose of food (which of course lightened my pack by a tiny but not to be underestimated 50 grams), we got up and began walking again and this time the atmosphere was more relaxed. The sun was shining and there was plenty more repellent left in the bottle. Then I heard concern in Georgina's voice.

'Err, where's the path?' she said and I peered over her shoulder to see the mud track come to an abrupt end and disappear into a mini ravine.

'Could we jump it?' I asked, but with a 3-metre gap it would have been a foolhardy move – even with Georgina's impeccable first-aid knowledge.

'There's nothing else for it, we'll have to walk down this way and see if there's a point where we can safely cross it,' I said, and began to wander along its crumbling lip. It seemed strange that it had suddenly ended – it didn't look natural and several steps later we hit a wide path covered in tarmac.

'Mmm, doesn't seem right.' I looked to see if there was any indication of it on the map. There wasn't.

It's difficult to explain why coming across a man-made road is so unnerving, but having been alone for several hours now, making our way through terrain that seemed akin to the Lost World, it felt like a real intrusion. Walking on it was odd and without realising it we had gone deathly silent. The main driveway continued on to a small homestead that sat a little way uphill. Its curtains were old and drawn shut in haphazard fashion – as if the occupants had closed them quickly. There was no sign of life and yet a sense of being watched.

I grabbed hold of Georgina's arm and she let out a scream. Without speaking, I gestured towards a dirt path that skirted the building, hidden somewhat by a line of trees. She composed herself and nodded and we walked hastily uphill and off the road treading carefully but with purpose. Then came the question.

'Is that a boot?'

I froze on the spot as the ramifications of what she was asking began to dawn on me and a whole tirade of questions came thick and fast in my head. Boot? What boot? Was there a person there? If there wasn't a person why a boot? And why only one and... oh my God was there a foot in it?!?

'Shhh!' was the only sound that came out my mouth. I suddenly felt like one of two clueless extras in the opening scenes of a movie and could almost hear the booming tones of the voiceover man: 'They thought they were taking an innocent hike. They thought they were alone. But in the woods... you never are...' Cue the roar of a chainsaw motor and the screams of the victims (me and Georgina) as we're chased by a maniac through the trees knowing that we're hours away from help. So much for all the confidence I'd built up on my solo adventures.

'Come on, don't just stand there,' I whispered, catching sight of the footwear. More and more walking gear seemed to be buried among the hardened mud: rucksacks, boots, tent poles.

'O God, O God, O God,' Georgina whispered as we climbed further up. Then I spotted something else – food containers, drinks bottles, sweet wrappers. This was a graveyard all right, but not for walkers who had lost their way, but for their rubbish. A dumping ground at the halfway point along the loch.

Relief gushed through me as I realised that the only criminals here were the ones who had trashed what would otherwise be a wild woodland. Even so, we cautiously tiptoed around the seemingly abandoned farmhouse, creeping past the outbuildings with perhaps a tiny part of us half expecting a lunatic to emerge at any moment.

We remained quiet for a while longer, following a new, much clearer path away from the buildings, until Georgina broke the silence, 'Intense that, wasn't it?'

'I won't even tell you what was going through my mind,' I chuckled as we began to spy the tops of a grand-looking building ahead. This was on the map – the Letterewe Estate – a huge manor house which our friendly cabbie had informed us the previous day, is hired out by rich parties (including 'that Martin Kemp from Spandau Ballet and *Eastenders*') for hunting. I spotted movement. A caretaker was moving something in the courtyard and stopped to look at us.

'The path goes that way, through the estate,' I said to Georgina as we felt his eyes burning into us.

'Well, I think they want us to go this way,' she pointed to a handpainted sign that directed us up through some overgrown woods. 'I don't think we are in a position to argue.'

Another man was down there now and they were staring in our direction. While we had every right to be there, still haunted by my thoughts from what I remember fondly as the walkers' burial ground, I fought my inner right of way campaigner and headed into the undergrowth once more. I even managed to fight the urge to swear when yet another branch slapped me in the face.

Emerging above the buildings the trees now began to thin and the track veered up. It had been a long day and the climb up of a few hundred metres felt like a mammoth undertaking.

'Nearly there I reckon,' I said optimistically, for about the fifth time, as we trod in the prints of quad bikes which had clearly been used by the estate on their stalking trips. Normally such tracks in a wild place as this would be offensive, but now they provided handy footholds in the otherwise slippery grass. Georgina was ignoring me. The first few times she had believed me but now she knew better. We plodded on. The slope seemed to go on forever. There was no sign of it relenting and like a cruel mirage, every time I felt the gradient ease, we would be met with more views of endless sloping grass. It was like being on an outdoor treadmill.

Suddenly and quite unexpectedly, my words finally became a reality and the path stopped climbing. We had topped out on the Bealach Mheinnidh, a saddle of land between two peaks. From here, the path descended into the valley where we needed to be. We looked at each other silently but I knew from her face that she had the same feeling of triumph that I did. Sun-drenched Fionn Loch sparkled hundreds of metres below our feet, with its neighbouring Dubh Loch appearing like a distorted reflection mirrored to its right. With craggy peaks rising on every side it was like passing through a gateway into a promised land. I felt like we were heroes returning to the homeland after a great and epic battle; I pictured myself as Christopher Lambert in *Highlander*, though perhaps without the strange accent.

It seemed so simple now and I told Georgina so. We just had to descend the path down to the water's edge, follow it across the causeway that cleaved the lochs in two and minutes later, we would arrive at our accommodation for the night. This was a barn that, a quick trawl through the internet will inform you, the estate kindly keeps open for walkers and climbers to spend the night in for free so that they can enjoy this patch of wilderness.

We started down the path, eager to tick off a successful first day. Despite tired legs we picked up the pace and it wasn't until I went to sip my water that I realised there was a problem.

'I'm out,' I said to Georgina gesturing at my hydration pouch.

'I was a while ago but didn't want to say,' she replied.

'No danger – I brought this!' Feeling a tad like Ray Mears, with a flourish I pulled a bottle out of my backpack that came complete with its own filter.

I filled it from the small waterfall that flowed by the side of the path, eager to feel the cold water in my mouth. But there was something I hadn't counted on. By the time the bulky filter system went back in the bottle it displaced all but a small mouthful of water, leaving very little inside left to drink – a definite design flaw if ever there was one.

'Problems?' mocked Georgina as I tried to suck some of the scant supply through the filter.

'Under control,' I lied, while just a tiny trickle spilled out. I handed it over to her and beamed with pride.

'I might wait till we get to the bothy and boil some instead,' she replied.

Dejected, I carried on my battle to extract drops of drinkable water from my useless contraption until we reached the causeway and, with hopes of the bothy ahead, I gave up. I knew it would be just over the next rise only a few minutes away. Besides, I was working up more of a thirst trying to get the bottle to dispense drink, losing more fluids in sweat than I was taking back in tiny globules of water.

A few minutes became five, then ten; fifteen minutes on, when Georgina asked me where exactly the bothy was, I began to think I was going insane.

'It's here on the map,' I said as my stomach leapt with a nervousness usually felt before the first drop on a rollercoaster.

I walked left, I walked right, I tried to get to high ground to find it. I couldn't understand where it could have gone. What I didn't realise was that while I was running around in all directions with all the level-headedness of a weeble, Georgina had continued on the path and was now trying to get my attention to let me know she had seen something.

'Look, look – ahead, AHEAD!' she gestured and I ran towards her. I squinted to see the roof of a large building. 'Is that it? It looks massive.'

As it was Georgina's first bothy, she sadly expected it to be something that grand. I avoided the question as we made our way to the gate. A sign read: 'Climbers and Hikers welcome to use barn 200 yards past house'.

'Ah... the barn,' she said. I nodded. 'Not the house.' I shook my head.

We walked towards it and I tried to squeeze the messages out of my head that I'd read on the walking forums in the weeks leading up to this trip, the ones that had decried it for being 'a wreck'.

When you approach a bothy there's always a level of apprehension that you feel opening the door. They are usually fairly small space-wise and there's always the chance that there won't be any room for you to stay there – sometimes even if there's only two other walkers inside. Standard practice recommends you always take a bivvy bag just in case so you can sleep outside. Thanks to Georgina, my pack was so full that I'd decided to ditch mine, so we were playing a game of sleeping roulette over the next two nights. Should this one be full I wasn't sure what to do next.

I braced myself and pushed the wooden door open with a loud creak. I nearly screamed. The skull of a Highland cow looked back at me from the wall. Gulping back the fear, I croaked 'empty' to Georgina and led the way inside. Though the smell was pretty rank, a kind of hybrid of damp hay and beer, it had one redeeming quality – a distinct lack of midges. Spiders had created a mass of webbing around any gaps by the roof making this an impenetrable fortress to the little biters. The floor was a bit of a disaster with stones broken and cracked, but thankfully we weren't relying on a flat surface because as luck would have it there were two bed frames that previous guests had covered with foam. Obviously if you went to stay at someone's house and they showed you this as a spare room you'd question your friendship, but believe me after walking as far as we had you'll sleep just about anywhere you can.

'I just hope no one else arrives,' pointed out Georgina, as there were only two beds. So in true childish fashion, after much debating and drawing of imaginary straws, we decided that one of us would stand guard over the bunks (Georgina) while the other (me) would go and collect water from the loch. I threw a mosquito net over my head and resembling some kind of crazy, sweaty beekeeper, I legged it to the shoreline. With mountains on all sides and no sign of roads or other people it felt like the quietest place on earth. We were truly in the wilderness. The only way to get into this peak-bordered valley was on foot and from either direction it was a long way. I could just about make out the peak that claims the title of Scotland's most remote Munro (although the definition of which one is the most remote is a contentious issue).

In a little under an hour we were fed, watered and knackered.

'What time is it?' I asked Georgina, as we both yawned. It felt like it was approaching midnight.

'Just coming up to nine,' she replied, 'I feel a bit old saying this, but I just want to sleep.'

That's the funny thing about walking and camping, time works differently away from houses and wall clocks. Here your body begins to get sleepy when the light in the sky begins to fade. With no *Corrie* or *X Factor* to keep you glued to the television while you were 'just flicking round' (I mean no one *really* watches these shows *on purpose* do they?), as the evening saps away, you actually go to sleep at a reasonable hour.

So at the positively civilised time of 9.15 p.m. we climbed into our respective beds and I waited to hear the usual sound of the mice scratching at the walls. I could hear Georgina's breathing begin to steady as she nodded off to sleep but feeling hot and restless, I lay there waiting for my tiredness to win its battle with the annoyingly alert side of my brain. Just as I'd dozed off, the sound of Georgina's voice brought me back to the here and now.

'Can you hear that noise?'

I mumbled something about the squeaky beds and turned over. Rabbit, sheep, cow, big cat, hound of the underworld... I had reached the point where I didn't care what was out there as long as I could sleep.

Another sound jarred me from my slumber and I woke to find that I'd turned over to face the cow skull. Georgina's voice was calling to me again, mumbling something about the location of the bathroom. In all my years of undertaking outdoor adventures the most common question I get asked is always some kind of variation on the old 'What do I do when I need the toilet?' conundrum. It's such a simple yet obvious problem for those only used to all mod cons complete with flush. Indeed it was one of my first questions when I started doing more overnight trips. The first time you pee outside is such a nerve-racking experience. No, perhaps I should rephrase that. The first time you pee outside *and you're a woman* is a nerve-racking experience. As we all know, men who have never even been in a wilderness situation will have relieved themselves in the great outdoors. In fact, many of us women have been inadvertent witnesses to it in many streets across the UK, nay the world. But for us, it's a fairly big deal. Sure there are SheWees (plastic devices that enable you to 'pee standing up', though take it from me they need some practice) but still, it's always going to be a slightly stressful experience. Then there's number twos.

With a kind of sadistic glee I turned to explain to Georgina just what the shovel in the corner of the bothy was for. 'You don't really use it though do you?' she asked after I finished. As I replied, I enjoyed her horror at my apparent uncouthness – up till this point I'm not sure I felt qualified to call myself an outdoors woman – but now it felt properly justified.

As she walked outside, visibly shaken by this revelation, I mused how this shovel-style toileting outside seems to be the last boundary before gaining full initiation into the outdoor world – there are many people I know for whom it took several trips before they could work up the courage to do it outside. After a few overnighters, though, I find you can have the opposite problem. You get so used to relieving yourself wherever you need to that if you feel the urge when out in town you start scouting hidden spots to 'go' and you actually have to remind yourself that it's not quite appropriate behaviour.

I tried to force myself back to sleep even though the call of nature was now shouting at me too. I lay there willing it to subside. I was feeling lazy, cocooned in my sleeping bag and I didn't want to do anything. This battle between mind and body went on for a while. It was taking place when Georgina came back inside, it was going on when she noisily clambered into her bed and still continuing when she'd dozed off with an enviable simplicity. We were at a stalemate. My body didn't want to let me rest and my mind refused to spur the whole process into action. It was at some point in this epic and timeless battle that my mind must actually have won and, without realising, I had fallen asleep. When blinding sunlight alerted me to the fact that it was morning, I tried to move and realised with a stab of pain that now I had to go to the toilet. Staggering out of my sleeping bag like a B-movie mummy I made my way to the door.

'Morning,' said Georgina and I barely waved in her direction as I hobbled outside.

When I finally returned, I found Georgina looking glum. I asked her what was wrong.

'Day two and already my electric toothbrush has run out!' she declared. I had to stop myself from hurling a tirade of abuse in her direction. Here I was, packing away her sleeping mat as she couldn't fit it in her miniscule pack, while she had had the audacity to bring an electric toothbrush.

It was a long day ahead of us and one that involved huge swathes of ascent to get to the next hut where we'd overnight. I'd planned a hike that would take us over the tops of three huge mountains – including the most remote one in the UK. To get there would require a climb up to the first summit before a tricky descent down to a col, another knee-busting ascent up to a ridge that we'd follow to the summit of the next peak. After that it would be another drop downhill, a skirt around another mountain's lower reaches then uphill again to the final high of the day. To end it all would be a big descent back down to the valley floor proper, then a meander along a river all the way to the second bothy, at the foot of the mighty An Teallach.

Even explaining it takes a lot of time so I was eager to get the day going. Taking the first path uphill, my legs already felt heavy due to the day before's activities and as I looked back and saw the bothy had disappeared back into the landscape below, I felt like our last link to civilisation had gone. It was both exciting and terrifying at the same time.

'We can cross the river there,' said Georgina, disturbing me from my thoughts, and I realised that we'd already reached Fuar Loch Mor where we needed to branch to the right to head towards A' Mhaighdean – the fabled, (supposedly) most remote mountain. Its top was already shrouded in cloud and as we edged the water to climb to the saddle, rain sprayed in our faces.

'Stay close, visibility is really decreasing,' I said to her as we donned waterproofs and began to climb up its vague path. Suddenly, as if hearing my warning, I couldn't see anything. Thick hill fog descended. It was all around, in front and to the sides, engulfing every sense. It was up my nose, in my ears, and in front of my eyes. I could feel the moisture from it with my fingertips and taste its musty flavour in my mouth. It was completely disorientating – like being in a whole lot of nothingness.

This wasn't the mountain to be on in thick fog; I knew for a fact it hid a network of cliffs, sudden drops abounded on its western edge and any false move could, quite realistically, see us plunging to our deaths. I had a secret weapon in the lid of my backpack though, yet another Ray Mears-style contraption. A GPS loaded with all the maps we would need and I produced it like an ace up my sleeve. I would use it to confirm our location and take a bearing to where we needed to head to.

Now technology is something I've never been that comfortable with when it comes to navigation; I remember one time relying on it on some moorland and having a raging row with it when it refused to cooperate with me. The number of times I've had a swearing match with the satnav in my car has reached triple figures (one time resulting in tearing it off the windscreen and swearing I would dump it at the next lay-by). So it was with some trepidation that I switched on the GPS and waited calmly for it to locate us. Five minutes later, we were still waiting; ten minutes and two chocolate bars and I was still none the wiser. By the time we edged the twenty-minute mark I flung it back into my bag with a flurry of expletives.

Luckily, in the time it had taken for my emergency electronic tool to fail me, the mist had thinned. Not cleared entirely but lightened enough that I could at least work out whether the ground under foot was solid and that we was not teetering on the brink of suicide.

'Do you feel like we're being watched?' asked Georgina and I followed her gaze to see a herd of deer, ghost-like on the edge of our visibility.

'They probably realised I was having a meltdown and came over for a better look,' I declared, more than a little put off by their ghoulish antlers silhouetted in the gloom.

We managed to feel our way to the summit cairn from where the ever-expanding views of nothing surrounded us. It did feel remote – but then you could be in the middle of a city in this weather and it would take on a very remote feel without much effort. I contemplated waiting for it to clear but the idea felt ridiculous. So we began to descend to the planned col, relying on a mix of visual clues and women's intuition. I had sworn off maps after the ordeal of trying to locate the bothy the day before, so felt my way off the slippery rocky ledges through a process of sliding on my bottom and keeping my fingers crossed. It seemed to take forever and by the time we reached our agreed stop point I was shaking.

'I say in this weather we should try to cut this way,' I said to Georgina, gesturing for us to continue at the height we were, ignoring the summit of the next peak completely. She agreed wholeheartedly, so tired that all she wanted to do was to be back inside the stone shelter of the night before.

We began walking, but the ground was deceptively uneven. Bog after bog sucked at our ankles. We were covering ground painfully slowly and I resigned myself to a life out here stuck on this saturated plateau with nothing but my broken GPS for company (Georgina was bound to have given up before me). Then a funny and rare thing happened. The sun broke through. Clouds began to break and dissipate. I could look back at the mountains and actually see the top of the peak were we'd just been. It was stunning, it was epic it was… infuriating! Why hadn't it done this when we were on the top of the mountain?

'We've got to gain some height and get back on the path,' I said as more beams of light sliced through the mist.

'You go on without me,' Georgina melodramatically pleaded, collapsing in a heap on the wet ground. My backpack had never felt so heavy and I could feel tears of frustration stinging my eyes but I knew we had to get up high. Summoning all my strength I grabbed Georgina's hand and started straight up towards the ridge, my thighs burning with every metre of ascent.

'What's that?' asked Georgina as she spotted a purple and yellow sheet flapping in the wind. I let go of her, pleased for a brief distraction and walked over to have a closer look. It was the sun-bleached fabric of a tent sheet, beside which was an equally bedraggled rucksack, ripped and weathered. This was obviously the spoils of another backpacker who had misguidedly stashed his kit on this complex ridge and had then been unable to relocate it, much like the gear we found in the 'walkers' graveyard' back near Letterewe. We continued upwards, Georgina moaning and I struggling to remain optimistic after seeing the failed attempt of a previous backpacker. Then, without pomp or ceremony, we were on the ridge. The views that greeted us were stupendous. Now I felt like crying, but this time for a good reason – this was probably one of the best views I've ever seen. Mountain after mountain curved round from our feet, radiating from the ridge we were standing on, each one majestic and jagged. Below, a network of rivers carved through the land creating a web of silver lines and opposite, the pinnacles and buttresses of An Teallach – one of Scotland's most prized peaks – glistened in the sunlight.

With tempers frayed and temperatures hotting up, reaching the top of that ridgeline had felt akin to scaling K2. My head was spinning as if I had a case of mild altitude sickness (I didn't of course). The hills that spilled out in every direction seemed Himalayan in stature and with my massive backpack, I felt like a Sherpa – not in the sense that I was badass at carrying heavy loads, but because my back felt like it was laden with enough stuff for a three-month expedition. But it's funny how on walks like this, the mud, sweat and tears can melt away and evaporate as if they'd never been there once you reach the top. A sit down, some water and a sneaky Jelly Baby (or twenty) can put the world to rights once more and, like a probably pinker version of the Duracell Bunny, I was filled with renewed energy and proceeded to lead the way.

'You've perked up, haven't you?' said Georgina as I strutted ahead on my 1,000-metre-high catwalk.

'I was fine the whole time,' I insisted, and left her shaking her head knowingly, as only real friends can get away with, as

I pulled myself up onto one of the many flat rock and grassy 'tabletops' that stud Beinn Tarsuinn. With warmth on our faces acting like a natural solar charger we were suddenly storming along and making fast progress. The views out to The Minch, the positively crown-like An Teallach, and the lochs and glens made me feel greedy at being able to see so much stunning landscape in a single eyeful. Any weariness from earlier had gone – I was hungry for more.

'Are we heading to the next bothy now?' asked Georgina as she looked at her watch – we were well into the afternoon.

'I think we should go and climb THAT first,' I replied, pointing at the tongue-twisting Mullach Coire Mhic Fhearchair – that for the purposes of being energy efficient with words will now be referred to as MCMF. It wasn't just the name that was tricky; to climb it from where we were meant a downclimb first then another upclimb of several hundred metres. I could see a shadow cast on Georgina's face and it wasn't from the clouds.

'Alright, you know best then,' she said and I walked on once more with purpose, trying to dismiss the extra kilometres as if they weren't even noticeable. The thing was, it had always been on the cards to go that way, but I wasn't going to let on to her that I had no idea how we'd reach the bothy from there. They don't call this area 'The Great Wilderness' for nothing. From where we were right along to the track that led to our chosen mountain hut, was a jigsaw of bogs, streams and miniature crags all designed to disorientate and sap strength from the eager adventurer.

Still, no point dwelling on the negatives I reasoned, so I put it to the back of my mind and led us up to the trig of MCMF. By the time we reached it, following a battle of wits and energy on a slope coated in spoils of slate like rocky hundreds and thousands, it was getting late.

'Are we going do the next one too?' asked Georgina in the tone of a woman who has been tricked one too many times.

'No, let's head down,' I said, desperately searched for an escape route off the mountain. The deer from earlier were further down the slope, looking at us in what I took to be a slightly goading manner, smug that they were nearly at the river which was our distant goal.

We moved on to the smaller summit to the east, where the stones seemed to suggest a way down on the scree. I went first and immediately regretted it as only several metres down, the small stones shot out from under my boots. Obviously eager to be eating food and stretching out in the comfort of a bothy and before I could express my concerns, Georgina was behind and coming at me – fast.

'Scree run!' she yelled as she passed by, diverting to the right and continuing down. A river of stone followed in her wake heading straight towards me. There was nothing for it but join in, so with a quick profanity yelled to help dispel the tension, I ran too screaming like a banshee.

Everything was moving fast, it was hard to keep up with the scenery passing before me. Every so often I made out the pink flash of Georgina's jacket which provided a handy marker, but other than that it was like a film reel moving far too fast to make sense. The rocks were getting deafening in my ears then suddenly I felt hands on my arms and a pulling sensation and I was flying through the air sideways. The crashing sound of the rockfall continued for several more seconds then slowed and stopped abruptly.

We had made it. Georgina had pulled me off it at the critical point so we could shelter from any free-flying shale behind a boulder. 'What now?' she asked.

With adrenaline pumping through me it took me a few seconds to work out where we were.

With my misguided 'not far now' assurance, we continued alongside the river heading downhill. I did foolishly think we'd managed an impressive amount of the descent already. It all seemed so simple until I noticed that the land either side of the water was getting higher while we was getting funnelled lower, being forced to scramble through the water. On a mission, I continued telling myself that it would all be over soon, until I heard a strange noise from above. It was familiar but what was it?

'Phoebe!' came a call. I was confused – who knew me out there? I looked behind to mention this oddity to Georgina and to my horror realised she wasn't actually behind me. I looked out above the water and back upstream but no sign. Then came the sound again.

I felt like I was going mad. I looked up. Standing at least 3 metres above, there she was. 'What the hell are you doing down there?' she asked laughing, 'I've been shouting at you for ages.'

'Get down here, this is the way,' I insisted.

'It's up here!' she yelled back and I could feel my face getting flushed with rage. I was tired, I was sick of the midges and more than all of that, I was hungry. Refusing to backtrack I clawed at the bank and hauled myself up, mud and soil covering my face as I went. As I reached the top, caked in dirt and knackered, I saw a recognisable feature – a whole network of granite slabs lying across the ground – almost like a bald patch in the grass. There was just one problem – how were we going to cross them? After a week of rain that had only ended the day before, they had been transformed into a slick, stone ice rink. This was beginning to feel like an assault course – both for the body and the mind.

'It's getting late,' said Georgina, as I gave up trying to walk across it on my feet and started shuffling sideways in a crab-like motion on my backside. My stomach was rumbling and I was hallucinating about a cold can of Cherry Coke which I had somehow convinced myself would be waiting for me if I could just get off the hill. Midges started to descend on us as we neared the stream, which thankfully was not in spate. Whilst Georgina found protruding stones on which to elegantly tiptoe across, I, being tired and a little fed up with carrying more than my fair share of my companion's load, waded on through, soaking my legs up to the knees while being eaten alive by the insects.

On the other side, I collapsed temporarily while Georgina filled her water bottle and I seriously considered sleeping right there and then. As my face was pressed against my encased map – a technique I'd inadvertently discovered for keeping at least one side of it from being bitten – I noticed the familiar square that denotes a building and by a pure stroke of luck, was only five little squares from the river where I currently lay. I felt better; we could make it and very soon would be snug indoors.

Now, you should know that five little squares on an Ordnance Survey map are actually 5 kilometres in real life. And although on a flat road it is an easy 45min amble, undulating up and down on a frankly bog-strewn track that resembled more of a river was far more epic... as we soon found out.

'How far did you say it was?' asked Georgina for the third time.

'I told you, five kilometres. I run more than that in thirty minutes. We'll be there any second now,' I replied as we began ascending yet another rise.

'Dear God – I hope that's not it,' said Georgina, pointing to pieces of corrugated iron rusted and torn in half lying in a haphazard fashion over a pile of old stones.

'Don't be ridiculous,' I said self-assuredly. Twenty minutes later, with still no sign of the bothy, I began to doubt myself.

It had become a marathon. Clearly the map was mistaken. Then the path disappeared. Now it felt like an Ironman event. Struggling to conceal my concern, I ploughed on through the increasingly muddy ground in robotic fashion, summoning all my strength to jump when it became a black stream of grime, and missing my landing more times than I made it. The sky was beginning to look as dark as the ground at my feet and I could tell by Georgina's pace that she must have a blister on at least one – if not both – feet. Whose idea was this bloody trip anyway?

Then I saw a sight that still ranks to this day as one of the best things I have ever witnessed. You can keep your ceiling of the Sistine Chapel, forget the majesty of a sunset and its shadow play on the orange sandstone of Uluru, and ignore the intricate decorative pelmets carved out of the mountains of Petra – the sight of the unassuming hut that is the Shenavall bothy outshone them all.

'Smoke,' said Georgina. After a moment of confusion where I nearly declined with a polite 'no thanks', I realised she was talking about the chimney. A wreath of white could just be made out wriggling its way out of the chimney. That could only mean one thing. We weren't alone.

'You go first,' urged Georgina and pushed me towards the door. I opened the creaky wooden door with an odd mix of sensations. On the one hand I was worried that we'd stumble upon a rowdy group of Glaswegians who'd nipped up for a night of debauchery fuelled by drugs and alcohol, and on the other hand I really didn't care so long as there was a corner where I could curl up and close my eyes.

'Hi,' came a male voice and I looked in to see a young, blonde man eating rice from a bowl. I felt like I'd inadvertently stumbled into every female walker's fantasy.

I looked to Georgina who had a grin on her face and immediately excused herself to walk into the other room.

I collapsed in a chair and began rooting around for my food, attempting to sound interested as Alex (who was from Poland), talked about his day whilst I struggled to even see straight. Minutes later Georgina came back into the room. For a woman who moments ago lacked the energy to fire up a camping stove, she had suddenly managed to muster a full outfit change and face of make-up. I wasn't sure whether to laugh at the ridiculousness of her flirtation or unleash a fit of rage, given that I had been hauling around half her kit in my bag, while she had secretly packed a change of clothes and an elaborate bath bag.

'I'm Georgina,' she said just as his blonde other half, Sylvia, entered the room to introduce herself. The glint in Georgina's eyes was immediately extinguished and was replaced once more with exhaustion. I couldn't stop giggling to the point where I think our bothy-mates assumed I was a tad unhinged.

We ate our food quickly and quietly while the pair recalled the adventure they'd had getting to this point. We would have joined in but I think were both too obsessed with our meals to bother. Finally, after passing around a Sigg bottle filled with whisky (classic bothy etiquette) we headed to one room, while they retired upstairs to the other. This was one of the oddest nights in my whole journey. Despite being in the middle of a mountainous heartland, to go from being alone, to having not just one but three other campmates and surrounded by the luxury of bricks, doors and log-burning fire of a house-type shelter, felt about as far removed from extreme as things could get. I felt strangely unadventurous.

Yet seeing the look of satisfaction and pride on Georgina's face as she began to drift off to sleep, and hearing her talk earlier with undoubted self-confidence to our bothy mates about what she'd done to get there, made me glow with the kind of pride a parent gets when seeing their child perform in a school play. While the expedition was no longer so extreme to me, it had clearly shown her a side to herself that she didn't know she had, and definitely proved that despite her reservations she could venture into the wild places and actually enjoy (at least parts) of the experience.

My tutelage may not always have been first class, but I hoped at least my passion for doing this had rubbed off on her... even just a little. Without much effort, I fell into a deep sleep to the soundtrack of cracking logs and light snores – which I'm not going to lie to you were probably mine.

Baaaaa! I opened my eyes. BAAAAAAA! I turned over, covered my head with my sleeping bag and fell right back to sleep.

Georgina and I slept in late. We lazily cooked a warm breakfast at 10 a.m. and were still eating and discussing how well we'd done the day before and how great the bothy was at 11 a.m.; I finally got dressed at 11.30 a.m. and at 12.30 p.m. following a session of taping up our feet with zinc oxide we were ready to move on. Today would be a shorter day, and by the end of it, we would leave the wilderness to be reunited with our car.

It had only been three days but we'd already reached that point where you can happily plod along without speaking. I've often noticed when multi-day walking that by day three your body has well and truly been beaten into submission and is working almost on autopilot. Day One is when it complains, aches and forces you to stop constantly to rest. Day Two is like the terrible twos are for kids – it actually rebels, unleashing a cascade of mini temper tantrums from spasms to profuse sweating and fits of unexplained rage. But by Day Three it's relented, surrendered to your cause and does what you tell it to do.

It's a great theory, but apparently no one had properly explained it to Georgina's body, which was already starting to break the rules. Each step seemed to her as much of a coordination nightmare as learning the tango. Her feet had become like giant clown feet tripping over each other as if rivals rather than teammates. As she nearly fell into a forward roll for what must have been the fifth time, I turned to ask if there was a problem.

'I've liked the wilderness, I really have,' she said, 'but I am really looking forward to getting back to civilisation.'

As we stumbled along the track which was losing signs of wild remoteness as we neared the hamlet ahead, we began to pass other walkers – a novel experience after the last three days. They looked squeaky clean and almost like a different species to us with our unkempt hair, dirty clothes and mud-encrusted fingernails. Though we must have only passed about six walkers in all, I felt like things were becoming crowded and as we emerged into Dundonnell and its one hotel, the car park was full with a coach load of tourists. I felt like we'd entered a metropolis. Georgina began to perk up, a wide grin on her face as she ran towards the toilet block screaming something about washing her hands and face and adding a line about popping into the nearby inn for a drink and cooked meal.

I smiled. I'd introduced her to my extreme sleeps but now she'd reached her limit. Not ready to give up just yet I had one final adventure left. As we supped on our drinks that night, Georgina listing all the things she couldn't wait to do back home – mainly involving a hot bath, clean clothes and her hair straighteners – I was already plotting my next escapade and, much like my introduction into all this wild camping, this one I needed to do by myself.

CHAPTER THIRTEEN

NORTHERN EXPOSURE

When it comes to Britain's most northerly point, John O'Groats is the headline stealer. Forget the fact that it's actually a piece of peninsula a further twenty minutes along the coast called Dunnet Head that claims the title, it doesn't matter. Because this place, perched on the northeast edge of Scotland is the kicking-off point for a multitude of charity bike rides to Land's End in the south (another tourist trap about 56 kilometres further west than the real southern extremity of Lizard Point). Whoever is or isn't the most northerly patch of ground is all fairly arbitrary it seems and any one of the places along the top edge of the country could have easily claimed the accolade had they fought hard enough for it. However in Scotland, for a taste of the truly unbridled north, the place that really does wipe the floor with its more media-savvy cousin, is over on the west. It's called Cape Wrath and is a jagged edge of Sutherland that reaches out into the North Atlantic

Ocean. Here are the highest sea cliffs in mainland Britain and a white lighthouse that shoots its beacon out to the rough and lonely sea. In summer, visitors head to Durness where you can take a ferry over the spit of water that makes direct road access impossible, from where you can catch a bus to the lighthouse café. Now, in winter, when it all shuts shop there's an even better alternative. Sandwood Bay. I was going instead to tackle the route on foot from the tiny community of Blairmore, ending just short of the lighthouse for one last wild sleep on my south-to-north adventure.

Around the time that Orwell sought escape from the rat race on Jura, and a little after Millican shunned the rat race in London for a simpler life in the Lakes, there was another man a couple of hundred miles away who was doing the same, though on a much more committed level. James McRory-Smith – or Sandy to his friends – decided that a simple life was definitely for him and set up home in an abandoned shepherd's hut that had been built around 1840 and sat a couple of kilometres from the shore of Sandwood beach. There he lived for over thirty years, making the 34-kilometre round trip walk to the nearest town for supplies and his pension every week, and living on a diet of fish, rabbits and deer that he caught out in his own wilderness. He died in 1999 and the bothy was taken over by the volunteer network of the Mountain Bothies Association that maintains shelters such as this one for walkers. He is long gone now, but some of his paintings still adorn the bothy walls and I desperately wanted to see them, to know what type of art work would come from a man who lived such an isolated existence for so long. I planned to walk to see his bothy and, depending on how kind the weather was, I would either stay there protected by the four walls around me or, as I hoped, pass back towards the bay and set up camp on the sand.

Getting to the start of my walk-in was a proper journey in itself. I'd thought the drive to Fisherfield was far, but from Dundonnell, I still had a few more hours to go before I would be anywhere near it. I chose the road that sticks near to the coast, weaving around the flat glens that suddenly made way for rising dome-like hills. Sprawling lochs, tumbledown castles and miles upon miles of rough and rugged terrain came into view and still I continued north. Signs punctuated the journey promising villages off more winding roads that disappeared behind sharp bends. The way ahead became increasingly narrow, with passing places strategically placed either side of the road to allow two vehicles to squeeze past each other. Finally, at length, I reached my exit from this endless tarmac strip.

I pulled into Blairmore. With all the time it had taken to reach here and tales of the deceptively hard 7-kilometre walk to Sandwood Bay, I wasted no time in sightseeing and rocked up into the car park, jumped out and made a beeline for the gate.

This route is known for being fairly dull, the main thing to recommend it is the promise of one of the most breath-taking beaches in Britain at the end. At first the track was easy, wide and well-used and led off into undulating moor, the grass either side proudly displaying its winterised coat. Despite a cold snap that had gripped this place a couple of weeks before my arrival, the temperature was up to double digits once more, holding at a steady 10°C. While it certainly wasn't warm, and the northerly wind gave it an undeniable nip, with a journey on foot ahead it seemed perfect for my purposes.

The first of several lochs appeared ahead, its water reflecting the muted grey tones from the sky above. I kept my head down and continued on my mission. Skirting the edge of the track, the sound of the loch's waves repeatedly thrashed against the sand in the driving wind. I was surrounded by some fairly wild scenery already, its taming given away only by the snaking trail I was walking on.

The ground began to get tough, rippling up and down with more rocks scattered across it. It took me back to the climb I'd taken to Castle Crag to find Millican's Cave, and I amused myself wondering how he and the elusive Sandy would have got on if they had ever met. Perhaps as two wilderness-lovers they would have had plenty to talk about and swapped storied about damp nights in leaky stone shelters; though I had read that Sandy liked a little of the Scottish tipple, and with Millican being teetotal, maybe they would have sat in stony silence, watching each other suspiciously, each doubting the other's credentials.

My imaginings helped pass the time and I realised with a soupçon of surprise that I had gradually climbed to a fair height, and the way ahead was starting to descend. I continued on, using the well-placed stepping stones to cross parts of the loch that had seeped outside of its boundary.

As I began climbing again, I could sense that my goal was in reach. Passing by the shell of an old bothy, now stripped of its roof, door and window, I picked up my pace excitedly, impatient for my first glimpse of the sea. The expansive freshwater Sandwood Loch, which feeds into the sea, emerged into view below. It looked like an ocean itself in size and it served to heighten my enthusiasm even more.

By the time I turned the corner I felt exasperated, irritated that the sea was still not visible. I ran downhill now towards the sheep that eyed me curiously from the long grass, before stopping dead in my tracks.

I've always thought of the Atlantic as a grey-green colour, like the water after washing dirty dishes. But now I could finally see it, it looked positively azure, crystal clear and so inviting. I had to fight a very strong urge not to go running for the breakwater. Now in winter, I might not be tempted to dive headfirst into it, but, as in Wales on my first solo trip, once more I found myself legging it down an incline, feeling a overwhelming torrent of elation intensifying in my stomach, adrenaline pulsing through me. I felt truly alive.

I stood for many minutes, more than likely with my mouth open, as Sandwood Bay exceeded every expectation I had built up in my head. Cliffs framed it on either side, creating a clear start and finish point, but it was wider than I believed it would feel from looking at the contours on the map. The sand was smooth and fine and virtually glowed pale white. A little further out, waves crashing against it, was the sea stack of Am Buachaille, a splinter of stone that stands almost at the height of the cliffs but sticks into the ocean floor bolt upright, an unclimbable tower (well unless you're pro-climbers Tom Patey and Ian Clough who were the first to scale it in 1968 that is). Its Gaelic name means 'the herdsman' and from where it was positioned, it did resemble a shepherd's crook and was doing a fine job of driving the sea into the inlet where I stood. Here, more stacks of rock acted like a natural breakwater as the sea crashed against them, frothing as it made contact with the stone.

Peering the other way, I could see the cliffs snaking off further north all the way to Cape Wrath where the fabled lighthouse was and a sheltered bay where the Vikings would turn their ships round before heading back to Norway. Closer to me, the chute of water that connected the loch to the mighty sea gushed and gurgled between pebbles.

It seemed funny that a place so beautiful had managed to escape having a main road to it. I guessed its northerly latitude was what had saved it from development and left it so perfectly unspoilt and spotlessly clean. I thought of more popular coastal areas around Britain, imagined this a victim of neon illuminations flashing along its edge, grand Victorian-style hotels blocking views of the moor, lochs filled in to make space for the coach parties. Whatever the reason, I was glad that for now it was safe.

I left this idyllic spot whilst I still had the willpower to do so. I was fast falling in love with its dunes and rocky slabs, wanted to linger, but I still had a bothy to check out. Strathchailleach was still a couple more kilometres over pathless rough ground. I'd spotted the shell of another building to the right of the track as I descended there and thought for a terrible minute I'd been misinformed and Sandy's bothy had gone. But it was simply an old farm building believed to be abandoned in the 1800s and fallen into disrepair. First the roof had gone, then the door, and slowly, piece-by-piece, the stones had tumbled down and nature won its battle with this man-made intrusion. Now the walls were only partially standing and grass covered their edges; the arches, still intact over empty windows, peered like soul-less eyes out into the landscape.

Crossing the water was trickier than I'd anticipated for it was not only fast-flowing, but deep too. I got wet feet making my way over, but feeling so good about this sleep I didn't care. The land was devoid of paths from that point and I climbed up once more using only deer and sheep prints to help guide me around the toughest lines of vertical rock. This next bit was not going to be easy I could tell, the ground became increasingly uneven and I knew that to reach the building meant a traverse over soggy heather-clad ground. I wasn't wrong.

As I avoided another bog and searched the landscape for another loch, I couldn't believe that an old man would have made this same journey almost daily, from house to sea, as a round trip to go fishing for trout at Sandwood Loch. In summer it might have seemed idyllic, but in the depths of winter it would have been a real chore.

The sky began to transform in colour as the sun began to slump down. The loch was finally ahead and I walked as quickly as I could in the muddy ground while some deer on the opposite side stared at this strange two-legged species invading their homeland. Several steps past the loch I spied a fence. Heading to it I was suddenly aware of more impenetrable inland peaks barring the way from the rest of Scotland like a fortress – a most effective deterrent.

Following the fence I came to a gate and after crossing it, as the land dipped down to a stream, I spotted the little red door and corrugated iron roof of the bothy. The stream that surrounded the little hut making it almost its own island, was where Sandy had sourced his water. From the land beneath my feet, he would collect peat to store for his fire as well as washed-up pieces of driftwood from the beach. He had no electricity or phone. When a gable collapsed he struck up a deal with the Mountain Bothies Association – they would repair it if he would allow walkers to stay in the front room, leaving him the one with a fire. He agreed, but stories of him locking the door or yelling at visitors rival the number of accounts of his welcoming nature.

As I reached for the door handle, I half expected to hear him roar at me to keep out – I held my breath for a split second, ready to dash away like a kid playing knock and run. But of course no sound came. I stepped into a little hallway first, then made a left turn into an empty room. There was a sleeping platform taking up much of the floorspace and a bottle with a candle stuck into it sitting in the window, but other than that, the room offered no glimpse into Sandy's life. I left this and walked back into the hall and through the door on the right of the entrance – now it felt like I'd stepped into a different building. It was like entering someone's home. I was struck immediately by the darkness and the strong odour of damp and old smoke. A couple of chairs filled the space in the middle of the room, a small shelf laden with books from previous visitors sat beneath a photograph of the man himself along with a description of him and his life. The fireplace was the main feature here, a set of bellows to the left to help burn the peat that was still stacked in piles by the side of the mantle. Everywhere on the walls were the paintings.

I moved closer to get a better look. They were mainly of animals, a horse, a bird and some more indecipherable critters on tiles. They were almost childlike in their style, he was certainly no Monet, but that made them all the more endearing. There was one in particular that caught my eye. It was of a woman playing a harp, a large image, her eyes staring at me from across the room, I didn't know who she was but I really felt like she was looking right into me. Feeling a little uncomfortable, I turned my back on it. There was one last door and this led into a much smaller room. In here were further paintings along with survival blankets and old food left from bothy users. For just a minute I swore

I could smell tobacco, but there was no one here but me – perhaps it was just a lingering smell from the past.

When Sandy got ill, much like Millican, he was taken to a hospital which is where he sadly died at the age of seventy-five and was buried in Sheigra a few miles away. He had once said that when he lived in the bothy his life was perfect: 'I want to live here forever' are his oft-quoted words, despite the hardships. It was such a shame that he never got to end his final years in a place he so loved.

I suddenly had a strong desire to leave. Being there in that place full of memories felt like an intrusion somehow, as if I was an uninvited guest in someone else's home. I looked out of the window to see the darkening sky. It was time to go.

I started retracing my steps back towards the sand. In the distance I could see a dot of light pinpricking the sky; the lighthouse had begun to fire up. Before it was built in 1828, there were a great many wrecks, but unlike the ships on the south coast which the locals managed to salvage parts from, most of the ships in this remote spot remained where they were, and it's odd to think that many of them are still buried underneath the sand. In the early 1900s the scene I was approaching would have resembled a boat graveyard with decaying hulls rotting away on the silt, waves crashing in through the portholes and spilling out onto the beach. About six years ago a local man in a light aircraft crash landed on this handy strip and escaped with no injuries. His plane, however, was a different story and it took fourteen men to come out and dismantle it so that they could remove the wreckage. It reminded me of Bleaklow, the wrecks perhaps not as obvious but lost underground, still there in spirit.

Finally I reached the beach and in the diminishing light, scanned for a pitch. I decided to nestle into one of the sand dunes, hoping that high tide would not sneak upon me in the middle of the night, waking me in a salty puddle.

The thing that always gets me about sand is how hard it actually is. When walking on it you can be deceived into believing that it's a very soft substance – this is a myth I'd like to dispel. As anyone who has slept on it will attest, sand is actually one of the hardest terrains to rest your head on. Your body weight compresses it like a memory foam mattress, leaving an imprint of your shape behind in it, but unlike that squidgy stuff, sand isn't so willing to shift so turning over can feel like taking a roll over concrete.

I found a section as soft as I was going to get. Although you should put the entrance to your tent away from the prevailing breeze, I pointed it firmly at the sea. There was no way I was going to miss having it as my view. The fabric flapped and fought against me as I tried to secure the outer sheet. I nearly became a walking human tent as a sudden gust wrapped it around me – this really was feeling like a two-person job. Finally I got the eyelet and the pole to connect and less than a minute later things were looking promising. As I untwisted the guy lines and fought to get the pegs to actually go in the sand – forgetting stupidly that soft sand means no grip – I remembered how excited and scared I'd felt back on my first solo sleep. Now I still felt the same enthusiasm but my fear had evolved, sure I remained occasionally jumpy, but now I was feeling something else, something that had slowly been creeping on over these adventures, but I was struggling to work out what it was.

The peg sprung out of the sand for about the fifth time, disturbing my thoughts. I needed to accept there was no way I could clamp the tent down here, I would have to rely on weights to secure it. Bored by thinking of practicalities in such a visually exquisite place I threw my rucksack onto its green belly and sauntered towards the water's edge. A movement on the cliffs caught my eye and I looked to see a sea eagle flapping its wings and pecking at its feathers. I watched it for a while, wishing I was small and agile enough to perch on such a ledge with waves crashing below me. About 8 kilometres away, Am Buchaille stood tall and blocky, uneven and precarious like an abandoned game of Jenga, as though any minute it might all fall down. The rocky shelf it sits on occasionally peeked out from the thrashing water. From here, for a split second it looked like a human form trying to swim against the current – my eyes as they always do, searching for a face in the darkness.

I wasn't the first to have spotted – or thought I spotted – something person-like out here. Back in the early 1900s a farmer called Alexander Gunn swore blind he saw a mermaid out on the rocks. He was walking with his dog, enjoying the fresh air, when his companion began to act very oddly indeed, growling and cringing in apparent terror.

It was at this point that old Alex saw the cause of such behaviour – a woman. At first he believed it to be a seal, not an uncommon sight in this part of the world, but then, with a growing sense of dread, he realised that it had hair – a mane of reddish yellow. Then he saw her eyes – deep blue-green like the sea that surrounded her, her 7-foot yellowish body stretched on a ledge above the tide. He claimed that she was trying to tempt him to come out to her, into the rough and lethal sea. Now while there are plenty of people for whom making up a story like this comes very naturally, locals in this area were adamant that Gunn was not one of them. More telling perhaps is that he never changed his account from when he first reported his sighting till the day he died in 1944.

It was likely a day much like it was now when this happened, the choppy sea, the stiff breeze, and the sky clear so you could make out such a deadly temptress. Seeing a mermaid would have been a highlight indeed. But all I could make out were endless upsurges, breakers and rollers, spiky rocks and a yellowy silt that stretched out from under my feet and disappeared off into the distance.

Chilled from my recollection of Alex's story and the difference the dropping sun was having on the temperature, I made my way back to the tent to find it on its side, my back pack having rolled down onto the wall and sand already beginning to reclaim it. The wind was sneaking into the gap between the inner and outer sheets, threatening to steal it off into the sky like a parachute. I would need to stay close so it didn't blow away and force me to seek refuge back in Sandy's bothy in the dark.

Pulling the tent over I felt the sting of the sand grains on my cheeks and battled with it a while to get it upright. This seemed to be the right time to start making some food, so I opened up my picnic. I noticed how the cover of my cooking pot had shrunk and blackened through over-use and felt like a hardened camper. I looked in either direction and was pleased to see no other person heading my way. It was nice to be so unconcerned about sleeping here compared with my covert operation at The Lizard, not having to stress over unpacking, keeping everything mobile should I be forced to move on sharpish. I deliberately took my time unpacking my sleeping kit as the sky made its final transition from day to night: my trusted warm sleeping bag, my battered sleeping mat and my shiny down jacket. I draped the bag around my shoulders and the jacket over my legs as I poured the steaming water into my mug. I was suddenly engulfed by warmth. The cocoa powder smelt alluring as I stirred it in and I waited with excitement while my food carried on cooking.

Looking out, the brightening moon was now reflecting off the rippling water, illuminating the beach with such a glow I didn't even need to get out my headtorch. Nestled in my little den of warmth, gazing out at the sea, without worry or care, I couldn't think of anywhere else I'd rather be. To think this had all begun to prove something to a bolshie Australian – it all seemed so insignificant now, but I was glad he had challenged me to seek these places out. I might never have found them otherwise.

I snuggled down further into my bag and lay on my tummy. I secured the tent door open with the bungy loops and spent several minutes gazing out at the sea. I really did understand why Sandy had said he wanted to live out here forever. Right now, given the choice between Uluru, Wadi Rum, Lapland, anywhere as a place I must remain indefinitely, I wouldn't have wanted to be anywhere but here. I wanted so much to stay awake, listening to the sounds of the sea, gazing out at the moon as it pulled the tides, and watching the light change as the hours passed. Instead I found that with my soothing sense of satisfaction and serenity, everything eventually faded to black and I dozed off to the roar of the sea and the flap of my tent with a sense of the contentment it seemed that I had been seeking the whole time.

When I woke up it was still dark; not because of a broken night but because at this time of year, everything stays dark until seven in the morning. I was sad to have missed the show but glad to have experienced a truly perfect extreme sleep. I sat up to see sand had crept into my tent during the night, caking the groundsheet with ochre. This was it.

I was desperately trying not to cry – but it wasn't easy. In front of me was the most overwhelmingly exquisite place I'd ever seen in my life. Waves, cliffs, sand, sea stacks, all placed so perfectly that I couldn't even in my wildest dreams have ever dared to hope that they actually existed in a reality –

and certainly not so close to home. All my previous sleeps came rushing back to me. I'd slept wild the entire length of Britain, from Lizard Point to this beach below Cape Wrath, and a smattering of landscapes in between. I'd proved that the wild places existed even on our small, well-populated island, and discovered landscapes in Britain that rival some of the best worldwide. I'd endured hard walk-ins, scrambles, rain, snow, fog, and now it all came down to this, one perfect moment.

I got out of my sleeping bag and ran to the edge of the shore. Staring out to sea I looked back to admire my footprints on the sand and watched as they slowly seemed to disappear, nature once more covering man-made tracks. With nowhere else to go, this would be the end of my extreme sleeps – at least for now.

Light was beginning to break, but it only revealed clouds moodily building above. I would have loved to have finished my journey bathed in sunshine, walking out of this untamed landscape like a hero in a blaze of glory. But endings are never as perfect as we'd like, otherwise I don't think we'd ever end anything. Yet this wasn't an ending, but a beginning, a jumping-off point to explore even more. I smiled, thinking of the ruined bothy being overcome by the undergrowth, the ships that had been reclaimed by the sand and the sea, the recalcitrant and uncontrollable sea. Staring at this scene that had so captured my heart I hoped that this would not be the last time I came here. I knew then that this would not be the end of my wild sleeps.

After packing away my kit and squeezing my tent into the bag, I began to lace up my boots, the last task needed before I would head home. I could feel the sand in them already, lining the bottom of my insole, permeating my socks and rubbing up against my toes. I didn't attempt to remove it by emptying out my footwear; instead I decided to take this little piece of wildness back home with me. In the weeks and months that followed, whenever I took out these boots, or erected that tent or even shook open my sleeping bag, I would be presented with a scattering of tawny coloured memories from this, my greatest adventure, enjoyed right here on the island I proudly call home. And that thought made me very happy indeed.

Inspired to get outdoors? Check out Phoebe's
must-have book before you go.

'Phoebe Smith is a splendid writer and an inspiring traveller'
Bill Bryson

WILD
NIGHTS

CAMPING BRITAIN'S
EXTREMES

PHOEBE SMITH

WILD NIGHTS
Camping Britain's Extremes

Phoebe Smith

£9.99

Paperback

ISBN: 978-1-84953-699-8

*As Phoebe Smith reveals, Britain is blessed with wilderness –
and you need no more than a tent and a misplaced sense of
confidence to experience it.*

Simon Calder

*... proves that you don't need to leave our own shores to
have some right royal muddy adventures in the UK.*

Julia Bradbury

Britain's most famous wild camper, Phoebe Smith, is back.
Battling whiteouts in Wales, facing monster waves in Suffolk
and making camp on Britain's highest mountain, Phoebe
takes us on a series of inspirational expeditions into the
wilderness as she quests to find the ultimate pitch.

Have you enjoyed this book?
If so, why not write a review on your favourite website?

If you're interested in finding out more about our books,
find us on Facebook at **Summersdale Publishers**
and follow us on Twitter at **@Summersdale**.

Thanks very much for buying this Summersdale book.

www.summersdale.com